Bass Theory

*The Electric Bass Guitar Player's Guide
to Music Theory*

John C. Goodman

Gneiss Press

For Heather
who made the journey
with me

Contents

Bass Theory

*The Electric Bass Guitar Player's Guide
to Music Theory*

"Everything is connected."

Introduction

The basics of music theory are not complicated or difficult to understand. Rather than think of it as music *theory*, think of it as music *knowledge*, knowledge of how music works, learning the mechanics of music the same way an automotive mechanic learns how a car engine works.

Music theory is highly patterned and once you understand the fundamental patterns, everything makes sense. The difficulty is in explaining the theory. In music theory, everything is connected. For example, you can't talk about chord tones without first understanding scales and scale degrees and intervals and keys and so much more. To grasp the basics it seems as if you have to grasp everything all at once and it can be overwhelming.

But if a car mechanic can learn about compression ratios and firing sequences and valve clearances, you can learn about intervals and scale degrees and modes. If you find it difficult, it is not because it is too hard for you, it's that it hasn't been explained in a way that makes it accessible to you. Don't give up.

There are no magic formulas or quick shortcuts, learning music theory requires study and thought and practice, but it can be very rewarding.

There are some contentious grey areas in music theory with different musicians taking different approaches resulting in disagreements between theory books. It may make things confusing when you are told different things by different people, but it is really a good thing as it shows that music theory is not a cut and dried fossilized system, but is a dynamic structure that grows and changes in accordance with the needs of music. Music theory is the trellis on which grows the flowering vine of music performance.

"Everything is connected."

Part I

Notes, Tones & Semitones

Notes

We will begin our journey into the fascinating and exciting world of music theory for the bass guitar with the **Note**. Notes are the basic building blocks of music, sort of like the atomic and sub-atomic particles.

Notes are named pitches. The Western or European tradition of music is based on seven tones, which are named after the first seven letters of the alphabet: A-B-C-D-E-F-G – always in capital letters. After G, the series repeats, with the next note after G being A: A-B-C-D-E-F-G-A-B-C-D··· etc. There are no H or K or M notes, only those seven letters are used. When the series repeats, it is called an Octave, so from A to A is one Octave.

Notes have:

- pitch; a frequency measured in hertz (hz)
- duration; how long the note is held
- volume; loudness or softness
- timbre; which is the tonal color or quality of a note; for example, on the electric bass, the position of the plucking hand relative to the bridge or neck changes the timbre or tonal quality of the played note.

Notes are written on the musical staff. There are two main staffs (or staves), the treble and the bass. The staffs are differentiated by symbols – called the treble clef and the bass clef. Melody is usually written on the treble staff and bass accompaniment on the bass staff. In between the treble and bass staves is Middle C, C_4 at 261.63 hz.

The range of an 88 key piano is just over 7 octaves, from low A_0 to high C_8, and most musical notation stays within this range. The A_4 above Middle C_4 was standardized at 440 hz in 1939, so 440 hz is always an A note (called Standard Pitch or Concert Pitch). Concert pitch is a relatively modern invention and before A 440 became standard there was a great deal of variation in tunings.

In sheet music, the bass guitar notes are an octave lower than the piano. For example, C on the bass staff

is played as C_3 on piano (130.8 hz), but played as C_2 (65.4 hz – the 3rd fret on the A string) on bass.

Besides pitch, notes have duration, they can be long or short. Written music is arranged into bars, or measures, with repeating patterns of beats, or pulses.

In North America we use a fractional note system. Even if you don't read music you will know these note durations because you have heard them in songs all your life. If a song is in common time, 4/4 with four beats to each measure, 1-2-3-4 | 1-2-3-4, then:

- a whole note is held for one bar, or a count of four
- a half note is held for a count of 2, with two half notes to a bar
- a quarter note is held for a count of one, with four quarter notes to a bar
- an eighth note is held for a half-beat, with eight notes to the bar, as in 1-and-2-and-3-and-4-and
- a sixteenth note is a sixteenth of a bar.

In the example above, the first bar shows a quarter note (one beat), an eighth note rest and an eighth note (2 eighths = 1 quarter note = 1 beat) and two more quarter notes for a total of four beats. The second bar shows 4 eighth notes (= 2 quarter notes = 2 beats) and a half note (= 2 beats) for a total of four beats to the bar.

In other time signatures, the notes retain these names. For example, 3/4 time has three beats to the measure, but the note is still called a quarter note even though there are three instead of four.

One thing that may be confusing is that the same letter can be used to mean several different things. We will get into the definitions further on, but it's helpful to know that a letter name, such as C can refer to:

- the note C
- the C major chord
- the root of the C chord
- the C major scale
- the tonic of the C scale
- the key of C

Any letter from A to G can refer to a note, a chord, a root, a scale, a tonic or a key – it's usually the context that tells us what meaning is being used.

When playing bass we play notes with pitch, duration, volume and quality. On the bass fingerboard, each fret is a unique note. We can find the A-B-C-D-E-F-G notes on the bass fretboard:

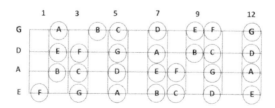

Tones and Semitones

The term **Tone** can be used in a few ways:

- a general term for a pitch. A note is a named pitch. You may hear tone and note used interchangeably informally, but 'tone' can refer to any pitch while 'note' refers to a specific pitch.
- a Whole Tone, the interval, or distance between two notes.
- timbre, the tonal color or tonal quality of a note. This sense is used when the EQ is adjusted to change the tone or when a bass player is described as having a unique tone.

Tones can be divided into **Semitones**, also called half-tones, half-steps, chromatic notes, accidentals or passing notes.

A semitone may refer to:

- a pitch between two notes
- the interval, or distance, of a half-step

A semitone is half a whole tone, so two semitones equal one whole tone. To move from note C to note D is to move one Whole Tone. The pitch between C and D is a semitone. Semitones are designated by sharps (#) or flats (♭). A sharp raises a note by a semitone, for example, C# is a semitone above C, falling between C and D. A flat lowers a note by a semitone, for example, D♭ is a semitone below D, falling between C and D. This results in each semitone having two names, for example, C# and D♭ are two names for the same pitch between the notes of C and D. Pitches with two names are called enharmonic.

It is important to understand how semitones are counted.

Semitones:	0	1	2
Notes:	C	C#/D♭	D
One Semitone	1/2 step		
One Semitone		1/2 step	
One Whole Tone (Two Semitones)	½ + ½ = 1		

There is only one pitch in between C and D, but the D note is counted as two semitones above C as it takes two half-steps to get from C to D – one half-step from C to C#/D♭ and one half-step from C#/D♭ to D; two half-steps equal one whole-step or whole tone.

On the bass fretboard, one fret is a semitone and two frets is a whole tone.

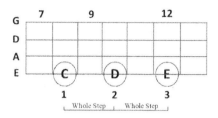

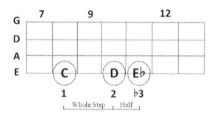

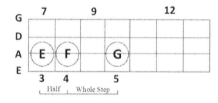

The C Major Scale

A scale is a series of ordered notes, as in the familiar *do-re-mi-fa-so-la-ti-do*. The first tone of the scale, 'do', is called the **Tonic** – that's tonic as in defining tone or tonal center, not an invigorating beverage like a spring tonic!

The tonal center of Western music is the C major scale, usually referred to simply as the C scale, consisting of seven pitches represented by the letters

C D E F G A B

This is called the **Diatonic Scale** (Diatonic is derived from an ancient Greek word meaning "passing tones" or "through tones").

Add another tonic, **C** D E F G A B **C**, and you have an eight note scale. Because there are eight notes, the interval, or distance, between the starting and ending notes of the scale, between the two tonics, is called an **octave** (from the Greek word for eight). An octave is the same note at a higher pitch – actually at double the frequency; for example, the C on third fret of the A string is C_2 at 65.406 hz, while the C an octave higher on the fifth fret of the G string is C_3 at 130.81 hz, exactly double the frequency.

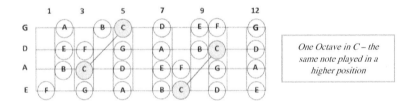

The scale is not restricted to eight pitches as the scale can be continued up or down by repeating octave notes:

C D E F G A B C D E F G A B C D E F G A B C···:‖ Repeat

Theoretically, the scale could go on repeating infinitely, but in reality it is limited by the range of notes available on musical instruments and/or the range of the human voice (and the range of the human ear!). The 4-string bass guitar, in standard tuning, starts on a low E_1 (the open E string at 41.20 hz) and continues on for several octaves. (The low B on a five string bass is B_0 at 30.87 hz.)

Scale Degrees

Understanding the C major scale provides a good basis for approaching all of Western music theory. In music theory, the notes of the scale are referred to by number, so for the C major scale:

1	2	3	4	5	6	7	8
C	D	E	F	G	A	B	C

The numbers used to designate notes are called **Scale Degrees**. The first note of the scale, the tonic, is counted as 1.

It may be obvious, but the letters of the alphabet and the scale degree numbers have nothing to do with the actual musical tones or pitches, they are simply convenient naming sequences.

The C Major Scale on the Bass Fretboard

We can find the C major diatonic scale on the bass fretboard:

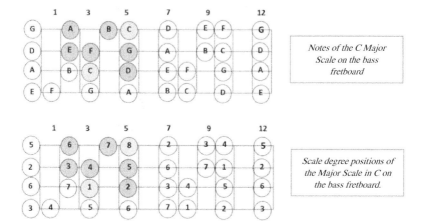

Notes of the C Major Scale on the bass fretboard

Scale degree positions of the Major Scale in C on the bass fretboard.

The Chromatic Scale

The natural notes of the C major diatonic scale are:

1	2	3	4	5	6	7	8
C	D	E	F	G	A	B	C

Between the natural (♮) tones of the scale there are semitones designated by sharps (#) or flats (♭). If we add the semitones to the diatonic scale, we get a complete scale of notes called the **Chromatic Scale**. In the chromatic scale, the distance between the tonic and the octave is divided into twelve equal semitones, called **equal temperament**. The chromatic scale in C is:

Diatonic Scale Degree:	1		2		3	4		5		6		7	8
Semitones:	0	1	2	3	4	5	6	7	8	9	10	11	12
Chromatic Scale:	C	C#/D♭	D	D#/E♭	E	F	F#/G♭	G	G#/A♭	A	A#/B♭	B	C

On the bass fretboard in C it looks like this:

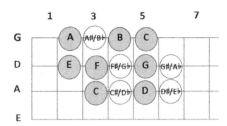

All music comes from the twelve notes of the chromatic scale. The chromatic scale can be repeated in successive octaves, but there are only those twelve notes. All the music you hear, from Bach to Taylor Swift is composed of those twelve notes. Every bass line ever composed, from the simplest to the most complex, is made from those twelve notes. The notes are fashioned into music through rhythm, melody and harmony.

The Major Scale Pattern

Notice that in the chromatic scale there are no sharp or flat notes (no semi-tones) between the notes B and C or between E and F. In these cases, B is the same as C♭ and C is the same as B♯; E is the same as F♭ and F is the same as E♯.

Diatonic Scale Degree:	1		2		3	4		5		6		7	8/1
Semitones:	0	1	2	3	4	5	6	7	8	9	10	11	12
Chromatic Scale:	C	C♯/D♭	D	D♯/E♭	E	F	F♯/G♭	G	G♯/A♭	A	A♯/B♭	B	C

The notes B and C, as well as E and F, are called natural notes and not accidentals even though they are separated by a half-tone instead of a whole tone. You can hear it in the scale *do-re-mi-fa-so-la-ti-do* – the third and fourth notes, *me-fa*, are a semitone apart, as are the *ti-do* seventh and eighth notes. The reason the scale is divided up this way goes all the way back to Ancient Greece with Pythagoras and his theory of perfect intervals.

Because of the natural half-tones in the scale we have a natural pattern of steps for the major scale of notes:

Chromatic Scale											
C	C♯/D♭	D	D♯/E♭	E	F	F♯/G♭	G	G♯/A♭	A	A♯/B♭	B	C
whole		whole		½	whole		whole		whole		½

The diatonic major scale pattern can be written as:

···**w-w-h-w-w-w-h**··· (w = whole tone; h = half tone).

1	2	3	4	5	6	7	8
C	D	E	F	G	A	B	C
w	w	h	w	w	w	h	

(In tables showing the step-pattern, like the one above, the steps show the distance between the notes. When a half-step "h" is shown under the F, it means that there is a half-step to the F from the *preceding* note, the E. The "w" under G means that there is a whole step to G from the *preceding* note, F.)

It is easy to remember the ···w-w-h-w-w-w-h··· major scale pattern as a series of half-steps if you think of it like a phone number: 221-2221.

Here is the C scale as a pattern of whole and half-steps on the fretboard, with each fret being a half-step and every two frets being a whole step.

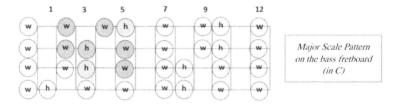

Major Scale Pattern on the bass fretboard (in C)

Knowing the major scale pattern of whole and half-steps is important; it is critical to understanding other scales, such as the minor scale, pentatonic scale, blues scale, etc., as well as modes, chords, and so much more.

Every note in the chromatic scale, including the semitones, can become the tonic of a new scale based on the major scale pattern. If we start with C we have a C major scale; if we start with D, using the same pattern, we have a D major scale; if we start with E♭, we have an E♭ major scale, etc.

Shown in the chromatic scale, the pattern of steps in C looks like this:

Scale Degree:	1	♭2	2	♭3	3	4	♭5	5	♯5/♭6	6	♭7	7	8
Chromatic Scale:	C	D♭	D	E♭	E	F	G♭	G	G♯/A♭	A	B♭	B	C
Chromatic Intervals:		h	h	h	h	h	h	h	h	h	h	h	h
Tonic Scale Intervals:			w		w	h		w		w		w	h

Although the semitones have two names, often one usage will predominate. The pitch between the scale degrees 1 and 2 is usually called a flat second (♭2) and the pitch between 2 and 3 is usually called the flat third (♭3). The ♭3 is used in the Minor Scale, in minor chords and diminished chords. The pitch between 4 and 5 is usually called flat five (♭5). The ♭5 is used in diminished chords and in the Blues Scale. (The ♭5 can also be called a ♯4 in augmented 4 chords.) The pitch between 5 and 6 is called sharp 5 (♯5) when used in augmented chords and flat six (♭6) when used in the Minor Scale. The pitch between 6 and 7 is called flat 7 (♭7). The ♭7 is used in dominant seventh chords, in the Minor Scale, the Minor Pentatonic Scale and in the Blues Scale.

The Bass Fretboard

The layout of notes on the bass fretboard (or fingerboard) follows the pattern of the C major scale. We have seen that in the C scale there is only a half-step between E and F, and between B and C, giving us the natural major scale pattern of whole steps and half steps, ···w-w-h-w-w-w-h···

That C scale pattern of notes with the half-step between E-F and B-C is the basis of the layout of notes on the bass fretboard. On the fretboard, each fret is a half-tone and every two frets is a whole tone.

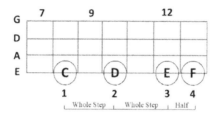

As you can see, on the fretboard E and F are right next to each other, a semitone apart, as are B and C, the way they naturally occur in the C major scale. All the other notes are two frets apart, or one whole tone.

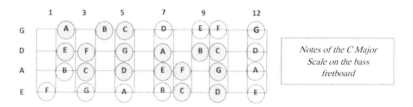

Notes of the C Major Scale on the bass fretboard

The notes on the 12th fret are the same notes as the open strings and after the 12th fret the pattern of notes repeats exactly. The twelfth fret is midway between the nut and bridge. At the midpoint of the string the frequency is doubled, and so note on the 12th fret is one octave higher than the open string.

The notes follow in order on each string, so a scale can be played by following the notes on one string:

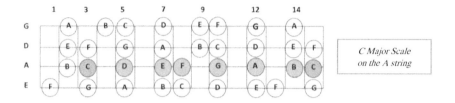

C Major Scale on the A string

The complete fretboard is the chromatic scale in the first 12 frets:

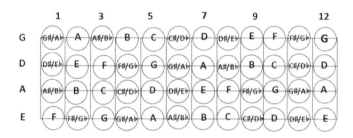

Learning the notes on the bass fretboard is essential. There are regular patterns on the fretboard that help us navigate around and stay oriented. If we know the notes of the open strings E-A-D-G, we can see that every time there is an E, there is an A above it; every time there is an A, there is a D above it; every D has a G above it.

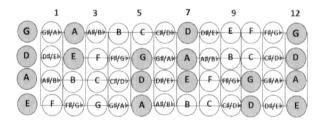

The half-steps in the C scale between E-F and B-C are always contiguous on the bass fretboard. Wherever there is a B-C together, E-F are on the next higher string.

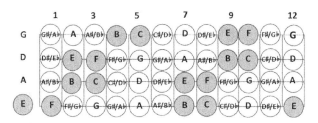

Counting the open strings, there are 48 notes in the first 11 frets, the 12 tones of the chromatic scale repeating four times.

The notes on the fretboard repeat in octaves. In the first eleven frets, every note occurs four times. There are four C notes:

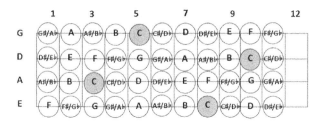

And four E notes (counting the open string):

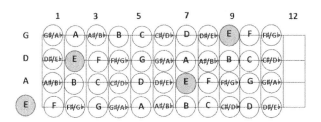

And the same follows for all the other notes on the fingerboard.

Because of octaves, the D string repeats the E string two frets up (for clarity, only the natural notes are shown, although the semitones repeat as well):

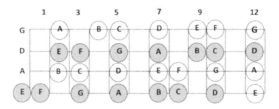

And the G string repeats the A string two frets up:

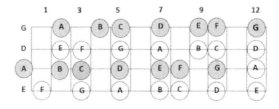

The fretboard is a series of repeating patterns. All this understanding of the fretboard layout gives us a good basis for learning the positions of the notes. The positions of the notes do not change, unless you change the tuning. The third fret on the lowest string is always a G; the fifth fret on the second lowest string is always a D. Once you learn them they aren't going to start shifting around on you.

Bass Tuning

In standard tuning, the bass is tuned in fourths with the open strings as E-A-D-G, the same tuning as the lowest four strings on a six-string guitar.

	E	F	G	A	B	C	D	E	F	G	
3 - D String							1	2	3	4	4 - G String
							D	E	F	G	
2 - A String				1	2	3	4				
				A	B	C	D				
1 - E String	1	2	3	4							
	E	F	G	A							

This may seem confusing, as the strings are tuned to the fifth fret on the fingerboard, but we are not counting frets, we are counting tones.

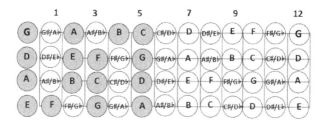

If we count the tones from the open E string, counting E as 1, we get E-F-G-A, four tones, which brings us to the 5th fret, so the open tuning of the next string is A. Starting from A, we get A-B-C-D, four tones, which brings us to the 5th fret, so the open tuning of the next string is D. D-E-F-G gives us four tones to the next string, G. Although we are on the fifth fret, we have moved up four tones, so the tuning is in fourths.

A six string bass has the highest string tuned to C, the fourth of the G string. A six string guitar has the 5th sting tuned to B, a third higher than the G string rather than a fourth. Most five string basses have a low B and high G, but some are tuned with a low E and high C. Four string basses can also be tuned B-E-A-D instead of E-A-D-G.

The double bass is also tuned in fourths as E-A-D-G, but the cello, viola and violin are tuned in fifths; G-D-A-E for the violin and C-G-D-A for the viola and cello.

The bass is called a C instrument or non-transposing instrument, as are the guitar, piano, violin, viola, cello, trombone, tuba, harp and flute. This means that a C on the bass staff is played as a C. We noted earlier that the C_3 on the bass staff is played C_2, an octave lower on the bass, but because the transposition is done in perfect octaves, the bass is still considered a non-transposing instrument (although some musicians class it as transposing).

Many instruments, especially brass and wind instruments, are transposing, which means that they are pitched to a key other than C, such as a B♭ clarinet or E♭ clarinet, a B♭ tenor sax, an E♭ alto sax or a B♭ trumpet.

The Minor Scale Pattern

After the Major Scale, the Minor Scale is next in importance. Every major scale has a relative minor. The relative minor uses the same notes as the major scale and has the same number of sharps or flats on the musical staff. The first note of the relative minor is the sixth note of the major scale. We know the scale degrees of the C major scale:

C	D	E	F	G	A	B	C
1	2	3	4	5	6	7	8/1

The sixth note is A, so the relative minor of C starts on A. Starting on A, the scale would be A-B-C-D-E-F-G. It works like this:

Scale Degree:	1	2	3	4	5	6	7	8/1	2	3	4	5	6	7
C Major Scale:	C	D	E	F	G	A	B	C	D	E	F	G	A	B
A Minor Scale:	C	D	E	F	G	A	B	C	D	E	F	G	A	B
Step-pattern:	h	w	w	h	w	w	w	h	w	w	h	w	w	w
	3	4	5	6	7	1	2	3	4	5	6	7	8/1	2

If we look at the step-pattern, we can see that when we start on A, the natural half-steps of B-C and E-F are shifted into different positions.

Chromatic Scale												
A	A#/Bb	B	C	C#/Db	D	D#/Eb	E	F	F#/Gb	G	G#/Ab	A
whole	½	whole		whole		½		whole		whole		

In the major scale, the half-steps are in the 3-4 and 7-8 positions, but in the minor scale, the half-steps are in the 2-3 and 5-6 positions.

Scale Degree:	1	2	3	4	5	6	7	8
Major Scale Pattern:		w	w	h	w	w	w	h
Minor Scale Pattern:		w	h	w	w	h	w	w

That is the difference between a major and a minor scale, the step-pattern. The minor scale pattern is:

···w-h-w-w-h-w-w··· (w = whole tone; h = half tone).

A scale that follows the ···w-h-w-w-h-w-w··· pattern is called a Natural Minor Scale. It is easy to remember the minor scale pattern as a series of half-steps if you think of it like a phone number: 212-2122.

We can find the Am scale on the bass fretboard:

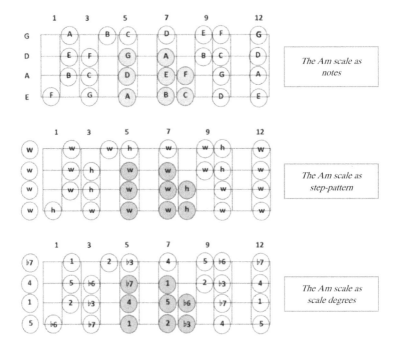

The Am scale as notes

The Am scale as step-pattern

The Am scale as scale degrees

Major and Minor Scale Patterns

The basic step-pattern is the same for both the major and minor scales, 2 whole steps followed by 3 whole steps separated by a half step, repeating over and over. This is the basic scale pattern.

···h-w-w-h-w-w-w-h-w-w-h-w-w-w-h-w-w-h-w-w-w-h-w-w-h···:‖ Repeat

If you cut out this chunk, you get a major scale:

···h-**w-w-h-w-w-w-h**-w-w-h-w-w-w-h-w-w-h-w-w-w-h···:‖ Repeat

If you cut out this chunk, you get a minor scale:

···h-w-w-h-w-w-**w-h-w-w-h-w-w**-w-h-w-w-h-w-w-w-h···:‖ Repeat

Every natural major scale and every natural minor scale has two half-steps. Because of the shift in position of the half-steps, when compared to the major scale, a minor scale can be said to have a flat 3rd, a flat 6th and a flat 7th. While the major scale has a whole step in the 2-3 position between D-E, the minor scale has a half step in the 2-3 position between B-C, resulting in a flat 3rd.

Major Scale Degree:	1	2	3	4	5	6	7	8
Major Scale Step-pattern:		w	w	h	w	w	w	h
C Major Scale:	C	D	E	F	G	A	B	C
Am Scale:	A	B	C	D	E	F	G	A
Minor Scale Step-pattern:		w	h	w	w	h	w	w
Minor Scale Degree:	1	2	♭3	4	5	♭6	♭7	8

The flat 3rd, flat 6th and flat 7th can be seen more clearly if we look at the Cm scale. The Am scale, starting on the 6th note of the major scale is called the Relative Minor. When a minor scale starts on the same tonic as the major scale, in this case C, it is called a Parallel Minor.

We know the step-pattern of the major scale:

1	2	3	4	5	6	7	8
	w	w	h	w	w	w	h

And we know the step-pattern of the minor scale:

1	2	♭3	4	5	♭6	♭7	8
	w	h	w	w	h	w	w

To make a Cm scale, we have to adjust the notes of the C major scale fit the step-pattern of the minor scale, and we do this using sharps or flats. The whole tone between D and E in the 2-3 position of the major scale has to be reduced to a half-step for the minor scale, so the E becomes an E♭, giving us a flat 3rd. The flat 3rd is the defining tone of a minor scale.

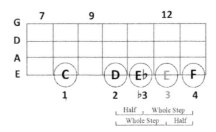

The sixth and seventh notes are similarly adjusted with flats to make the scale conform to the minor scale pattern. Our whole Cm scale will look like this:

Major Scale Degree:	1	2	3	4	5	6	7	8
Major Scale Step-pattern:		w	w	h	w	w	w	h
C Major Scale:	C	D	E	F	G	A	B	C
Cm Scale:	C	D	E♭	F	G	A♭	B♭	C
Minor Scale Step-pattern:		w	h	w	w	h	w	w
Minor Scale Degree:	1	2	♭3	4	5	♭6	♭7	8

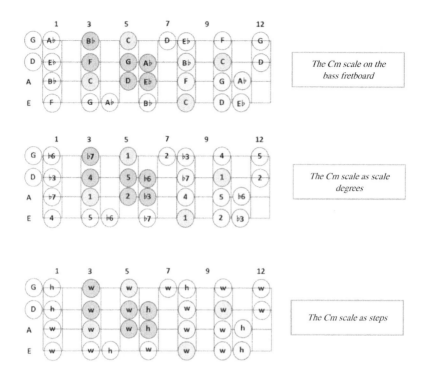

The Cm scale on the bass fretboard

The Cm scale as scale degrees

The Cm scale as steps

The Cm scale starts on C, the same as the C major scale. It does not start on Cm – there is no C minor note. Notes can be natural (♮), sharp (#) or flat (♭), but not major or minor.

In looking at the C, Cm and Am scales, we have introduced the notion of **Keys**.

Keys

The C major, Am and Cm scales we have looked at are all in different **Keys**.

A scale is a sequence of notes. The key covers the scales, the chords, melody, and everything else that can be created from the scale notes.

The name of the key is determined by the starting note of the scale, so if the scale starts on C, it is the key of C with the scale C D E F G A B C; if you start with A, then you are in the key of A; if you start with E, you are in the key of E; and so on. Any note in the chromatic scale can be used as the starting note for a key. The starting note is called the Keynote.

The notes of the chromatic scale are:

Chromatic Scale:	C	C#/Db	D	D#/Eb	E	F	F#/Gb	G	G#/Ab	A	A#/Bb	B

The Chromatic Scale gives us 17 possible major keys.

	1	2/3	4	5/6	7	8	9/10	11	12/13	14	15/16	17
Chromatic Scale:	C	C#/Db	D	D#/Eb	E	F	F#/Gb	G	G#/Ab	A	A#/Bb	B

As every major key has a relative minor, there are also 17 possible minor keys. To say that the key is determined by the starting note of the scale is a working definition, but the key in music is defined by the number of sharps and flats in the scale, as shown on the musical staff, called the Key Signature. The C major scale has no sharp or flat notes, but the Cm scale has three flats:

C Major Scale:	C	D	E	F	G	A	B	C
Cm Scale:	C	D	Eb	F	G	Ab	Bb	C

On the bass staff, the key signature for Cm would look like this, with three flats:

As Cm is the relative minor of Eb (which means that C is the sixth note of the Eb scale) , the key signature of three flats signifies both Eb and Cm.

Each key has a unique signature and it is the number of sharps or flats that differentiates one key from another. There are several reasons why we use different keys. One reason is vocal range – a baritone will require a different key than a tenor or a soprano. You can see in the graphic below the different range of notes available in different keys:

A piece may be set in a key that makes the fingering easier for the solo instrument, such as the guitar, keyboard or saxophone. Songs are written in a specific key, but musicians performing covers of a song do not have to stick with the original composer's key.

Different keys have different tone-colors or flavors, which communicate different moods. Songs will often be composed in a key that the writer feels complements the mood or emotional tone of the melody. Some people find major keys have a happier, brighter, more positive sound while minor keys have a sadder, darker, more melancholy emotional tone.

The keys of C♯, D♯, G♯, and A♯ are rarely used, giving us thirteen common major keys:

1	2	3	4	5	6	7/8	9	10	11	12	13
C	D♭	D	E♭	E	F	F♯/G♭	G	A♭	A	B♭	B

Because the semitones have two names, their keys can be written in two ways, for example, F♯ is the same as G♭. These are called Enharmonic keys.

Every major key has a relative minor key.

Major Key:	C	D♭	D	E♭	E	F	F♯/G♭	G	A♭	A	B♭	B
Relative Minor:	Am	B♭m	Bm	Cm	C♯m	Dm	D♯m/E♭m	Em	Fm	F♯m	Gm	G♯m

The keys of A#m, Abm, B#m and E#m are rarely used, giving us thirteen common minor keys (D#m and Ebm are Enharmonic keys.):

1	2	3	4	5	6	7/8	9	10	11	12	13
Am	Bbm	Bm	Cm	C#m	Dm	D#m/ Ebm	Em	Fm	F#m	Gm	G#m

Some keys have an unmanageable number of sharps or flats and are called Theoretical Keys. You can see in the table of major keys that there is an Eb, but no enharmonic D#; this is because the key of D# has nine sharps, which makes it rather complicated, and so it is not used. You may also notice that in the table of minor keys there is a D#m; why is there a D#m key, but no D# major key? It is because D#m is not a minor form of D# major; D#m is the relative minor of F# and so shares the same notes and same number of sharps as the key of F# major (6 sharps).

There are keys with up to nine sharps or flats, but they are rarely used. They do sometimes show up in popular music, for example, *Born Under a Bad Sign* by Booker T. Jones and William Bell, a hit for Albert King, and Hoagy Carmichael's *The Nearness of You*, performed by Ella Fitzgerald, are in C#, a key signature with 7 sharps.

The most common keys in popular music are G, C, D, A and E, along with their relative minors, Em, Am, Bm, F#m and C#m – those ten keys will get you through most popular music. Add F, Ab, Bb and Eb, and their relative minors, Dm, Fm, Cm, and Gm, for a total of eighteen common keys and you will have most of everything covered.

Keys tend to be grouped according to the style of music or instruments used. Common keys for C instruments like guitar and piano (or keyboard) are C, E, A, D and G, along with their relative minors.

Common keys for arrangements with transposing instruments often used in jazz, like the Eb alto saxophone or Bb trumpets, are Bb, Eb and F, along with their relative minors. Blues numbers often straddle rock and jazz. A lot of Chicago blues music is guitar based so G, C, D, A and E and their relative minors are common blues keys. Memphis blues and Jump blues, which incorporate horn sections, often use keys such as Ab or Eb.

But these are just tendencies; there are no restrictions on what keys can be used for which style of music and you will find music of all kinds of styles written in all kinds of keys.

Major Scales

Every key has a unique scale of notes, and all are based on the pattern of the C major scale. The notes of the C major scale are C-D-E-F-G-A-B and the step-pattern is ···w-w-h-w-w-w-h··· with natural half-steps between E-F and between B-C.

Scale Degree:	1	2	3	4	5	6	7	8
C Major Scale:	C	D	E	F	G	A	B	C
Step-pattern:		w	w	h	w	w	w	h

We know the pattern of the C major scale on the bass fretboard:

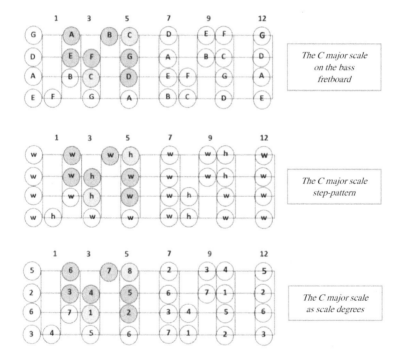

The C major scale on the bass fretboard

The C major scale step-pattern

The C major scale as scale degrees

All of the major scales of the thirteen common keys follow the same step-pattern as the C major scale. Whatever note you start on, you will always sing *do-re-mi-fa-so-la-ti-do*.[1]

If we start our scale on D, the notes are D-E-F-G-A-B-C, but this does not conform to the major scale step-pattern:

Major Scale Degree:	1	2	3	4	5	6	7	8
Major Scale Step-pattern:		w	w	h	w	w	w	h
D:	D	E	F	G	A	B	C	D
D Step-pattern:		w	h	w	w	w	h	w

As you can see, the natural sequence of D-E-F-G-A-B-C with half-steps between E-F and B-C puts the half-steps in the wrong place for the major scale pattern. In the major scale, there is a half-step between scale degrees 3-4, but when we start on D, the natural half-step between E-F falls in the 2-3 position (this is actually called the Dorian Mode, but it's not the major scale). To force the D notes to conform to the major scale pattern, we need to adjust the notes using sharps.

We need a whole step between degrees 2-3, so we adjust the F up a semitone to F♯; this puts the half-step between F♯ and G in the correct 3-4 position. We also need a half-step in the 7-8 position. The natural half-step between B-C falls into the 6-7 position, so we move the C up a semitone to C♯, giving us a whole step between B-C♯ in the 6-7 position and a half-step between C♯-D in the 7-8 position.

Our adjusted D scale looks like this:

Major Scale Degree:	1	2	3	4	5	6	7	8
Major Scale Step-pattern:		w	w	h	w	w	w	h
D Major Scale:	D	E	F♯	G	A	B	C♯	D

---

[1] Using syllables for notes is called Solmization. The system using *do-re-mi-fa-so-la-ti-do* is called solfège. There are different forms of solfège, using various syllables, such as *sol* for *so* or *si* for *ti*. Movable *do* solfège uses the syllables for the tonic in any key, but in fixed *do* solfège *do* is always C.

The D major scale thus has two sharps – and that is how the Key Signature is shown on the bass staff:

This is why all major scales, except C, have sharps or flats, because the note intervals have been adjusted to conform to the major scale step-pattern, the basic pattern of whole steps and half-steps of the C major scale.

On the bass fretboard, the notes of the D major scale follow the same step-pattern as the C major scale:

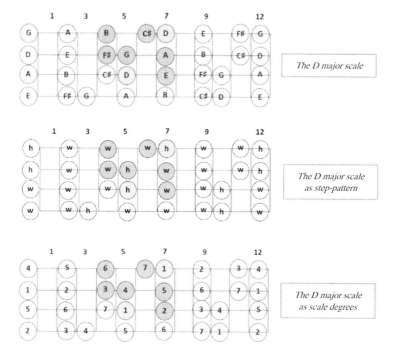

The pattern of the steps and half-steps remains the same for every major scale in every key. Whatever note we start on, the half-steps are adjusted with sharps and flats to force the scale to conform to the step-pattern of the C major scale.

Sharps and Flats in Major Scales

Some scales use sharps to adjust the intervals, the steps between notes, to fit the C major scale pattern, and some use flats. The reason is because in some keys the intervals have to be adjusted up, and in others they have to be adjusted down. Each sharp or flat adjusts a note by one semitone.

We have seen how the intervals had to be adjusted up using sharps in the D major scale:

Major Scale Degree:	1	2	3	4	5	6	7	8
Major Scale Step-pattern:		w	w	h	w	w	w	h
D Major Scale:	D	E	F#	G	A	B	C#	D

But when we look at the F major scale we find:

Major Scale Degree:	1	2	3	4	5	6	7	8
Major Scale Step-pattern:		w	w	h	w	w	w	h
F:	F	G	A	B	C	D	E	F
F Step-pattern:		w	w	w	h	w	w	h

In F, the natural half-step between E-F falls in the 7-8 scale degree position, right where it is supposed to be for the major scale pattern. But the B-C half-step falls in the 4-5 position and we need to move the half-step to the 3-4 position; we do this by lowering the B a semitone to B♭, which gives us a half-step between A-B♭ in the 3-4 position and a whole step between B♭ and C in the 4-5 position. The step-pattern of F now conforms to the major scale pattern.

Major Scale Degree:	1	2	3	4	5	6	7	8
Major Scale Step-pattern:		w	w	h	w	w	w	h
F Major Scale:	F	G	A	B♭	C	D	E	F

In D, the natural half-step between E-F fell in the 2-3 position and we had to move it up to the 3-4 position using a sharp. In F, the natural half-step between B-C fell in 4-5 position and we had to move it down to the 3-4 position using a flat. Every major key moves the half-steps into the 3-4 and 7-8 scale degree positions and sometimes you need sharps and sometimes flats.

One thing to notice is that scales have either sharps or flats, not both. You won't find mixed scales with some notes sharp and others flat (except in special circumstances).

Major Scales in Thirteen keys

Here is the Major scale in thirteen keys:

Steps:		w	w	h	w	w	w	h
Degree:	1	2	3	4	5	6	7	8
C	C	D	E	F	G	A	B	C
Db	Db	Eb	F	Gb	Ab	Bb	C	Db
D	D	E	F♯	G	A	B	C♯	D
Eb	Eb	F	G	Ab	Bb	C	D	Eb
E	E	F♯	G♯	A	B	C♯	D♯	E
F	F	G	A	Bb	C	D	E	F
F♯	F♯	G♯	A♯	B	C♯	D♯	E♯	F♯
Gb	Gb	Ab	Bb	Cb	Db	Eb	F	Gb
G	G	A	B	C	D	E	F♯	G
Ab	Ab	Bb	C	Db	Eb	F	G	Ab
A	A	B	C♯	D	E	F♯	G♯	A
Bb	Bb	C	D	Eb	F	G	A	Bb
B	B	C♯	D♯	E	F♯	G♯	A♯	B

F♯ and Gb are enharmonic keys, they have the same number of sharps and flats; F♯ has six sharps and Gb has six flats. They share the same pitches, but in the F♯ scale the step-pattern is expressed in sharps and the Gb scale uses flats.

Notice that in F♯ the seventh note is an E♯ – an E♯ is an F. In Gb the fourth note is Cb – Cb is B. Why are they called E♯ and Cb instead of F and B? For a few reasons.

Let's look at where the half-steps fall in the scale.

Major Scale Degree:	1	2	3	4	5	6	7	8
Major Scale Step-pattern:		w	w	h	w	w	w	h
G major Scale:	G	A	B	C	D	E	F♯	G
G Step-pattern:		w	w	h	w	w	w	h
G♭ major Scale:	G♭	A♭	B♭	C♭	D♭	E♭	F	G♭
G♭ Step-pattern:		w	w	h	w	w	w	h

The G♭ scale is a half-step below G, so all the notes have to be adjusted accordingly to fit the major scale step-pattern. When the B is lowered to B♭, it leaves a whole step between B♭ and C, so the C must be lowered to C♭ for the half-step between degrees 3-4. It's called C♭ instead of B because the B note is already flat, so there is no B♮ in the scale.

We can see this in the key signature for G♭ on the bass staff:

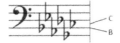

The second line B already has a flat on it, so the only way to show that the C (second space on the staff) is lowered is to add a flat.

Because of this, there is a rule that scales can't have two notes with the same letter name, such as B and B♭. That doesn't mean that you can't use two notes with the same letter name; for example, if you are in the key of C and walkup from C to G, you might play, 1-3-4-5♭-5, C-E-F-G♭-G, and have both G and G♭, but the G♭ is an accidental, it is not a scale note of the C scale – it's only scale notes that cannot have the same letter name.

The same reasons apply to the E♯ in the F♯ scale – E♯ is the same pitch as F♮, but in the F♯ scale it is called E♯.

The way the sharp and flat notes are built in scales results in some scales having double sharps (𝄪) and double flats (♭♭) to show that we are dealing with raised or lowered notes, not natural notes.

The sharps and flats in the scales follow a pattern. The major sharp keys are:

Key	1	2	3	4	5	6	7		-
C	C	D	E	F	G	A	B	No Sharps	
G	G	A	B	C	D	E	F♯	1 Sharp	F♯
D	D	E	F♯	G	A	B	C♯	2 Sharps	F♯-C♯
A	A	B	C♯	D	E	F♯	G♯	3 Sharps	F♯-C♯-G♯
E	E	F♯	G♯	A	B	C♯	D♯	4 Sharps	F♯-C♯-G♯-D♯
B	B	C♯	D♯	E	F♯	G♯	A♯	5 Sharps	F♯-C♯-G♯-D♯-A♯
F♯	F♯	G♯	A♯	B	C♯	D♯	E♯	6 Sharps	F♯-C♯-G♯-D♯-A♯-E♯

Notice that each new key adds one sharp, building in a regular pattern on the previous key with F♯, then C♯, then G♯, then D♯, then A♯, then E♯. We don't find one key with C♯-A♯-E♯ and another with G♯-D♯-E♯.

The major flat keys are:

Key	1	2	3	4	5	6	7		
C	C	D	E	F	G	A	B	No Flats	
F	F	G	A	B♭	C	D	E	1 Flat	B♭
B♭	B♭	C	D	E♭	F	G	A	2 Flats	B♭-E♭
E♭	E♭	F	G	A♭	B♭	C	D	3 Flats	B♭-E♭-A♭
A♭	A♭	B♭	C	D♭	E♭	F	G	4 Flats	B♭-E♭-A♭-D♭
D♭	D♭	E♭	F	G♭	A♭	B♭	C	5 Flats	B♭-E♭-A♭-D♭-G♭
G♭	G♭	A♭	B♭	C♭	D♭	E♭	F	6 Flats	B♭-E♭-A♭-D♭-G♭-C♭

As with the sharps, the flat keys build in a regular pattern, starting with B♭, then E♭, then A♭, then D♭, then G♭, then C♭.

Every sharp added changes the key by a fifth. The key of C has no sharps, but add a sharp and the key is G. G is the fifth note of the C scale. Add another sharp and the key is D. D is the fifth note of the G scale, etc.

Every flat added changes the key by a fourth. C has no flats; add one flat and the key is F. F is the fourth of the C scale. Add another flat and the key is B♭. B♭ is the fourth note of the F scale, etc.

Minor Scales

Every major key has a relative minor and the relative minor is a key of its own. We have seen how the relative minor is derived from the 6th degree of the major scale:

Scale Degree:	1	2	3	4	5	6	7	1	2	3	4	5	6	7
C Major Scale:	C	D	E	F	G	A	B	C	D	E	F	G	A	B
A Minor Scale:	C	D	E	F	G	A	B	C	D	E	F	G	A	B
Step-pattern:		w	w	h	w	w	w	h	w	w	h	w	w	w

Starting on the 6th note of the major scale gives us a new step-pattern: ···w-h-w-w-h-w-w··· This is the minor scale pattern and it is the step-pattern that distinguishes minor scales from major scales.

The relative minor of C major is Am. The Am starts on the A note and uses the same notes as the C scale. The tonic of the Am scale is A, not Am – there is no Am note, notes can be natural (♮), sharp (♯) or flat (♭), but not major or minor – it is the scale that is minor, not the note. Because the step-pattern is different, when compared to the major scale the minor scale can be said to have a flat 3rd, flat 6th and flat 7th.

Major Scale Degree:	1	2	3	4	5	6	7	8
Major Scale Step-pattern:		w	w	h	w	w	w	h
Minor Scale Step-pattern:		w	h	w	w	h	w	w
Minor Scale Degree:	1	2	♭3	4	5	♭6	♭7	8

With the major scale, we saw how the diatonic scales in all other keys used the same step-pattern as the C major scale. Similarly with the minor scale, the diatonic scale in all other keys uses the same step-pattern as Am.

All minor scales have exactly the same shape on the bass fretboard, only the position changes:

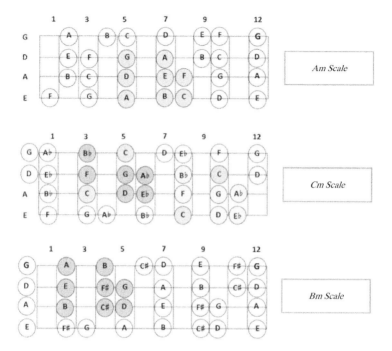

Relative Minors

Here are thirteen Major keys and their Relative Minors (F♯/G♭ are enharmonic keys):

Major Key:	C	D♭	D	E♭	E	F	F♯/G♭	G	A♭	A	B♭	B
Relative Minor:	Am	B♭m	Bm	Cm	C♯m	Dm	D♯m/E♭m	Em	Fm	F♯m	Gm	G♯m

It is easy to find the Relative Minor for any Major key on the bass fretboard, just find the 6th of the scale.

C Scale:	C	D	E	F	G	A	B	C
Major Scale Degree:	1	2	3	4	5	6	7	8

The simplest way is to go one string lower to the 5th and up two frets to the 6th. The graphic shows the scale degrees in C. For every tonic 1 (C), the 5th (G) is on the next lowest string, and two frets up from the 5th (G) is the 6th (A), so in C the relative minor will be Am.

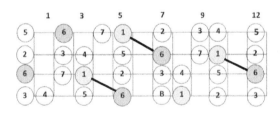

Another way to find the relative minor is to count down three notes from the octave of the major scale:

Major Scale Degree:	1	2	3	4	5	6	7	8
C Scale:	C	D	E	F	G	A	B	C
						3	2	1

38

If you are in a minor key and want to know the Relative Major, the Relative Major is always the ♭3 of the minor scale, so just count up from the tonic to the flat 3rd. The Relative Major to Am is C.

Am Scale:	A	B	C	D	E	F	G	A
Minor Scale Degree:	1	2	♭3	4	5	♭6	♭7	8

On the bass fretboard it looks like this (for Am):

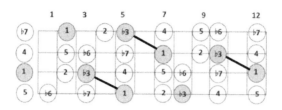

This works for all minor scales.

Sharps and Flats in Minor Scales

Minor scales have the same number of sharps or flats as their Relative Majors. We can see this in the D major and Bm scales:

Scale Degree:	1	2	3	4	5	6	7	1	2	3	4	5	6	7
D Major Scale:	D	E	F♯	G	A	B	C♯	D	E	F♯	G	A	B	C♯
B Minor Scale:	D	E	F♯	G	A	B	C♯	D	E	F♯	G	A	B	C♯
Step-pattern:	h	w	w	h	w	w	w	h	w	w	h	w	w	w
Minor Scale Degree:	♭3	4	5	♭6	♭7	1	2	♭3	4	5	♭6	♭7	1	2

The sixth degree of the D major scale is B, so our relative minor is Bm. The Bm scale has the same two sharps, C♯ and F♯, as D major. This is why the major and relative minor can share the same key signature. The key signature with two sharps is both D major and Bm.

Because the minor scale is derived from the major scale, we get the same distribution of sharp keys and flat keys.

The sharp minor keys are:

	1	2	♭3	4	5	♭6	♭7		
Am	A	B	C	D	E	F	G	No Sharps	
Em	E	F♯	G	A	B	C	D	1 Sharp	F♯
Bm	B	C♯	D	E	F♯	G	A	2 Sharps	F♯-C♯
F♯m	F♯	G♯	A	B	C♯	D	E	3 Sharps	F♯-C♯-G♯
C♯m	C♯	D♯	E	F♯	G♯	A	B	4 Sharps	F♯-C♯-G♯-D♯
G♯m	G♯	A♯	B	C♯	D♯	E	F♯	5 Sharps	F♯-C♯-G♯-D♯-A♯
D♯m	D♯	E♯	F♯	G♯	A♯	B	C♯	6 Sharps	F♯-C♯-G♯-D♯-A♯-E♯

The flat minor keys are:

	1	2	b3	4	5	b6	b7		
Am	A	B	C	D	E	F	G	No Flats	
Dm	D	E	F	G	A	Bb	C	1 Flat	Bb
Gm	G	A	Bb	C	D	Eb	F	2 Flats	Bb-Eb
Cm	C	D	Eb	F	G	Ab	Bb	3 Flats	Bb-Eb-Ab
Fm	F	G	Ab	Bb	C	Db	Eb	4 Flats	Bb-Eb-Ab-Db
Bbm	Bb	C	Db	Eb	F	Gb	Ab	5 Flats	Bb-Eb-Ab-Db-Gb
Ebm	Eb	F	Gb	Ab	Bb	Cb	Db	6 Flats	Bb-Eb-Ab-Db-Gb-Cb

As with the major keys, every flat changes the key by a fourth and every sharp changes the key by a fifth.

Minor Scales in Thirteen keys

Here are the minor scales in thirteen keys:

		w	h	w	w	h	w	w
Degrees:	1	2	b3	4	5	b6	b7	8
Am	A	B	C	D	E	F	G	A
Bbm	Bb	C	Db	Eb	F	Gb	Ab	Bb
Bm	B	C#	D	E	F#	G	A	B
Cm	C	D	Eb	F	G	Ab	Bb	C
C#m	C#	D#	E	F#	G#	A	B	C#
Dm	D	E	F	G	A	Bb	C	D
D#m	D#	E#	F#	G#	A#	B	C#	D#
Ebm	Eb	F	Gb	Ab	Bb	Cb	Db	Eb
Em	E	F#	G	A	B	C	D	E
Fm	F	G	Ab	Bb	C	Db	Eb	F
F#m	F#	G#	A	B	C#	D	E	F#
Gm	G	A	Bb	C	D	Eb	F	G
G#m	G#	A#	B	C#	D#	E	F#	G#

D♯m and E♭m are enharmonic keys, they use the same notes, but expressed as sharps in D♯m and as flats in E♭m. In Dm, there is an E♯, which is the same pitch as F♮, and in Em there is a C♭, which is the same pitch as B♮ – they are written as E♯ and C♭ for the same reasons as the G♭ and F♯ major scales.

More Scales

There are six basic scales that are important to know:

- the chromatic scale
- the major scale
- the minor scale
- the major pentatonic scale
- the minor pentatonic scale
- the blues scale.

In addition, there are other minor scales, such as the harmonic minor and melodic minor, as well as the Dominant scales. We have covered the chromatic, the major and the minor scales, so let's look at the others.

Major Pentatonic Scale

Derived from the major scale, the major Pentatonic uses only 5 notes, the 1-2-3-5-6 of the scale. Pentatonic comes from the Greek word for five.

Scale Degrees:	1	2	3	4	5	6	7	8
C Major scale:	C	D	E	F	G	A	B	C
C Major Pentatonic Scale:	C	D	E		G	A		

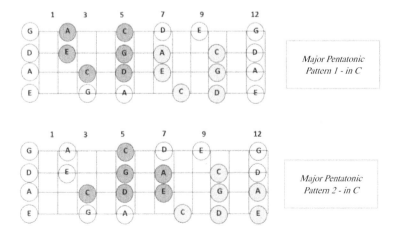

Major Pentatonic
Pattern 1 - in C

Major Pentatonic
Pattern 2 - in C

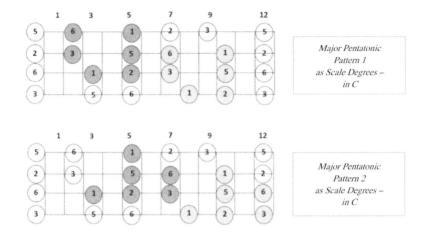

The Major Pentatonic in Thirteen Keys

Degrees:	1	2	3	5	6	8
C	C	D	E	G	A	C
Db	Db	Eb	F	Ab	Bb	Db
D	D	E	F#	A	B	D
Eb	Eb	F	G	Bb	C	Eb
E	E	F#	G#	B	C#	E
F	F	G	A	C	D	F
F#	F#	G#	A#	C#	D#	F#
Gb	Gb	Ab	Bb	Db	Eb	Gb
G	G	A	B	D	E	G
Ab	Ab	Bb	C	Eb	F	Ab
A	A	B	C#	E	F#	A
Bb	Bb	C	D	F	G	Bb
B	B	C#	D#	F#	G#	B

F# and Gb are enharmonic.

Minor Pentatonic Scale

The minor Pentatonic scale is a five note scale derived from the natural minor scale, using the 1-♭3-4-5-♭7. The minor pentatonic is widely used in blues and rock as it can be played over major chords, especially dominant 7 chords.

Scale Degrees:	1	2	♭3	4	5	♭6	♭7	8
A minor scale:	A	B	C	D	E	F	G	A
Am Pentatonic Scale:	A		C	D	E		G	

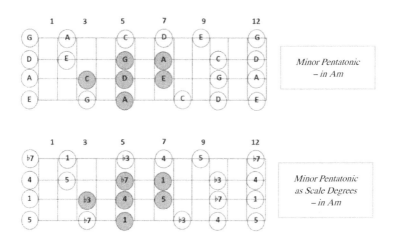

Minor Pentatonic – in Am

Minor Pentatonic as Scale Degrees – in Am

The Minor Pentatonic in Thirteen Keys

Degrees:	1	b3	4	5	b7	8
Cm	C	Eb	F	G	Bb	C
C#m	C#	E	F#	G#	B	C#
Dm	D	F	G	A	C	D
D#m	D#	F#	G#	A#	C#	D#
Ebm	Eb	Gb	Ab	Bb	Db	Eb
Em	E	G	A	B	D	E
Fm	F	Ab	Bb	C	Eb	F
F#m	F#	A	B	C#	E	F#
Gm	G	Bb	C	D	F	G
G#m	G#	B	C#	D#	F#	G#
Am	A	C	D	E	G	A
Bbm	Bb	Db	Eb	F	Ab	Bb
Bm	B	D	E	F#	A	B

D#m and Ebm are enharmonic.

46

The Blues Scale

The Blues Scale is a 6 note scale similar to the minor pentatonic scale, but with the addition of a ♭5, giving us a diminished fifth. The degrees of the blues scale are 1-♭3-4-♭5-5-♭7.

Scale Degrees:	1	2	♭3	4	♭5	5	♭6	♭7
A minor scale:	A	B	C	D		E	F	G
A minor Pentatonic:	A		C	D		E		G
A Blues Scale:	A		C	D	E♭	E		G

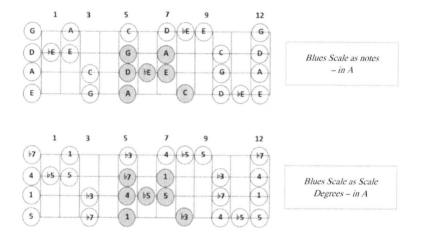

Blues Scale as notes – in A

Blues Scale as Scale Degrees – in A

Although it has the flat, or minor, third, the blues scale is unique and is not usually referred to as a minor scale.

The Blues Scale in Thirteen Keys

Degrees:	1	b3	4	b5	5	b7	8
C	C	Eb	F	Gb	G	Bb	C
Db	Db	E	Gb	G	Ab	B	Db
D	D	F	G	Ab	A	C	D
Eb	Eb	Gb	Ab	A	Bb	Db	Eb
E	E	G	A	Bb	B	D	E
F	F	Ab	Bb	B	C	Eb	F
F#	F#	A	B	C	C#	E	F#
Gb	Gb	A	B	C	Db	E	Gb
G	G	Bb	C	Db	D	F	G
Ab	Ab	B	Db	D	Eb	Gb	Ab
A	A	C	D	Eb	E	G	A
Bb	Bb	Db	Eb	E	F	Ab	Bb
B	B	D	E	F	F#	A	B

F# and Gb are enharmonic.

Harmonic and Melodic Minor

There are many variations of the natural minor scale; the two most common are the harmonic and melodic minor scales. The natural minor scale has a ♭3, ♭6 and ♭7. The alternate minor scales are made by making some of these flat notes natural (♮), or substituting major intervals for minor intervals – except for the ♭3 which is the defining tone of a minor scale.

Harmonic Minor

The **Harmonic Minor scale** uses a natural 7th instead of a flatted 7th; which means it uses the same seventh note as the major scale. This scale is used when the melody encourages a smoother transition from the 7 to the tonic, or to cover a minor chord with a major 7th, such as a CmM7. The 7th note of the scale is called a Leading Tone or Tendency Tone because it tends to lead the ear back to the tonic.

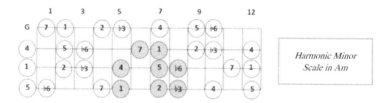

Harmonic Minor
Scale in Am

This solves one of the difficulties with minor scales. In the major scale, the seventh note is called the Leading Tone because it feels like it wants to resolve upwards and return to the tonic. The minor scale with the flat seven lacks that strong leading tone. What the harmonic minor does is move the seventh up a half-step closer to the octave tonic to provide a leading tone to take the ear back to the tonic. The step-pattern of the Harmonic minor results in a one-and-a-half step interval from the ♭6 to the major 7.

	1	2	♭3	4	5	♭6	7	8
Am	A	B	C	D	E	F	G♯	A
		w	h	w	w	h	wh	h

Harmonic Minor Scale in Thirteen Keys:

Degrees:	1	2	♭3	4	5	♭6	7	8
Cm	C	D	E♭	F	G	A♭	B	C
C#m	C#	D#	E	F#	G#	A	B#	C#
Dm	D	E	F	G	A	B♭	D♭	D
D#m	D#	E#	F#	G#	A#	B	C##	D#
E♭m	E♭	F	G♭	A♭	B♭	C♭	D	E♭
Em	E	F#	G	A	B	C	D#	E
Fm	F	G	A♭	B♭	C	D♭	E	F
F#m	F#	G#	A	B	C#	D	E#	F#
Gm	G	A	B♭	C	D	E♭	G♭	G
G#m	G#	A#	B	C#	D#	E	F##	G#
Am	A	B	C	D	E	F	G#	A
Bm	B	C#	D	E	F#	G	A#	B
B♭m	B♭	C	D♭	E♭	F	G♭	A	B♭

D#m and E♭m are enharmonic.

Raising the 7th a semitone results in some enharmonic notes. In C#m, the B# is the same as C; in D#m and F#m, E# is the same as F; and in E♭m, C♭ is the same as B. We also have some double sharps: C## in the D#m harmonic minor scale and F## in G#m. C## is enharmonic to D and F## is enharmonic to G, but they are written as double sharps because we are actually dealing with a double raised C and F. They have the same pitch as D and G, but different names because of the scale intervals. Double sharps are indicated in sheet music with an 𝄪 symbol.

There is a problem in the Dm harmonic minor: we have both a D and a D♭, breaking the rule of never having two tones with the same letter name in any one scale. We could call the D♭ a C#, but Dm is a flat key (relative minor of F major), so a sharp is out of place – and we have a B♭ in the ♭6 position, so adding a C# would be mixing flats and sharps in the same scale, breaking another rule. Breaking the rules is unavoidable in this case, but music theory is adaptable.

Melodic Minor

The **Melodic Minor scale**, sometimes called the Jazz Minor, is different going up and coming down. Going up, the melodic minor has a flat 3rd, but natural 6th and 7th notes. Coming down, the natural minor scale is used, with the flat 3rd, flat 6th and flat 7th. (The same melodic minor pattern can be used both ascending and descending, but the natural minor is commonly used for descending.)

The Ascending Melodic Minor provides the major 7 leading tone and solves a melodic problem of the harmonic minor with the awkward-sounding one and a half steps between the ♭6 and the major 7.

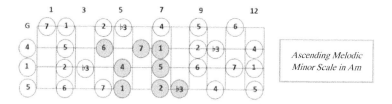

Ascending Melodic Minor Scale in Am

The Melodic minor ascending is the same as a major scale with a flatted third. The flat third is a defining tone of the minor scales, so even though the 6 and 7 are natural, it is still called a minor scale.

	1	2	♭3	4	5	6	7	8
Am	A	B	C	D	E	F♯	G♯	A
	w	h	w	w	w	w	h	

Melodic Minor Scale in Thirteen Keys:

	Melodic Minor Ascending								Natural Minor Descending						
	1	2	b3	4	5	6	7	8	b7	b6	5	4	b3	2	1
Cm	C	D	Eb	F	G	A	B	C	Bb	Ab	G	F	Eb	D	C
C#m	C#	D#	E	F#	G#	A#	B#	C#	B	A	G#	F#	E	D#	C#
Dm	D	E	F	G	A	B	C#	D	C	Bb	A	G	F	E	D
D#m	D#	E#	F#	G#	A#	B#	C##	D#	C#	B	A#	G#	F#	E#	D#
Ebm	Eb	F	Gb	Ab	Bb	C	D	Eb	Db	Cb	Bb	Ab	Gb	F	Eb
Em	E	F#	G	A	B	C#	D#	E	D	C	B	A	G	F#	E
Fm	F	G	Ab	Bb	C	D	E	F	Eb	Db	C	Bb	Ab	G	F
F#m	F#	G#	A	B	C#	D#	E#	F#	E	D	C#	B	A	G#	F#
Gm	G	A	Bb	C	D	E	F#	G	F	Eb	D	C	Bb	A	G
G#m	G#	A#	B	C#	D#	E#	F##	G#	F#	E	D#	C#	B	A#	G#
Am	A	B	C	D	E	F#	G#	A	G	F	E	D	C	B	A
Bbm	Bb	C	Db	Eb	F	G	A	Bb	Ab	Gb	F	Eb	Db	C	Bb
Bm	B	C#	D	E	F#	G#	A#	B	A	G	F#	E	D	C#	B

D# and Eb are enharmonic.

Raising the flat six and seven to natural six and seven results in a number of enharmonic notes:

In C#m, B# is the same as C.

In D#m, E# is the same as F; B# is C; C## is D.

In Ebm, Cb is the same as B.

In F#m, E# is the same as F.

In G#m, E# is the same as F; F## is G.

Dominant Scales

Dominant scales are tied to Dominant 7th chords. Understanding Dominant scales now will help in understanding the structure of the chords later, as well as secondary dominants and modal interchange.

Each degree of the scale has a name. We are already familiar with the initial tone, the Tonic. The other degrees are:

1	Tonic
2	Supertonic
3/♭3	Mediant
4	Subdominant
5	Dominant
6/♭6	Sub-mediant
♭7	Subtonic
7	Leading

The fifth note of the scale is called the Dominant because of its harmonic relationship to the tonic, the Perfect ratio of 3:2, as we can hear when we play roots and fifths – we don't often play root and fourth, or root and sixth, we play root and fifth.

We know that minor scales use the same notes as major scales, but start on the 6th note of the root scale. Here is the F major scale and the relative D minor:

Scale Degree:	1	2	3	4	5	6	7	8/1	2	3	4	5	6	7
F Major Scale:	F	G	A	B♭	C	D	E	F	G	A	B♭	C	D	E
D Minor Scale:						D	E	F	G	A	B♭	C	D	
Scale Degree:						1	2	♭3	4	5	♭6	♭7	8/1	

In the same way, we can derive scales that start on another scale degree, but still use the notes of the root scale. The 5th degree of the scale is called the Dominant, so if we start our scale on the 5th, we will have a Dominant Scale:

Scale Degree:	1	2	3	4	5	6	7	8/1	2	3	4	5	6
F Major Scale:	F	G	A	B♭	C	D	E	F	G	A	B♭	C	D
C Dominant Scale:					C	D	E	F	G	A	B♭	C	
Scale Degree:					1	2	3	4	5	6	♭7	8/1	

53

Although our Dominant scale starts on C, it is not a C major scale because it uses the notes of the F scale. The difference between the C major scale and the C Dominant scale is the B♭.

Scale Degree:	1	2	3	4	5	6	7	8/1
C Major Scale:	C	D	E	F	G	A	B	C
C Dominant Scale:	C	D	E	F	G	A	B♭	C

The Dominant scale has its own step-pattern:

Root Scale Degree:	1	2	3	4	5	6	7	8/1	2	3	4	5	6	7	8
Dominant Scale Degree:					1	2	3	4	5	6	♭7	8			
F major scale:	F	G	A	B♭	C	D	E	F	G	A	B♭	C	D	E	F
Step-Pattern:		w	w	h	w	w	w	h	w	w	h	w	w	w	h

Notice that with the Dominant scale we are using the same recurring scale pattern with a different chunk cut out:

···w-w-h-w-**w-w-h-w-w-h-w**-w-w-h-w-w-h-w-w-w-h-w-w-h···:‖ Repeat

Using the Dominant scale shifts the half-step from the 7-8 position of the major scale to the 6-7 position, resulting in a flat 7.

Scale Degree:	1	2	3	4	5	6	7	8
C Major Scale:	C	D	E	F	G	A	B	C
C Major Step-pattern:		w	w	h	w	w	w	h
C Dominant Step-pattern:		w	w	h	w	w	h	w
C Dominant Scale (from F):	C	D	E	F	G	A	B♭	C
Scale Degree:	1	2	3	4	5	6	♭7	8

In the Dominant scale, the 7 is not flat, it is a natural half-step note. However, when compared to the C major scale, the C Dominant scale can be said to have a ♭7.

Scale Degree:	1	2	3	4	5	6	7	8/1
C Major Scale:	C	D	E	F	G	A	B	C
C Dominant Scale:	C	D	E	F	G	A	B♭	C
Scale Degree:	1	2	3	4	5	6	♭7	8/1

Dominant Scales in Thirteen Keys

Root Scale:	1	2	3	4	5	6	7	8/1	2	3	4	5
					1	2	3	4	5	6	b7	8
C	C	D	E	F	G	A	B	C	D	E	F	G
Db	Db	Eb	F	Gb	Ab	Bb	C	Db	Eb	F	Gb	Ab
D	D	E	F#	G	A	B	C#	D	E	F#	G	A
Eb	Eb	F	G	Ab	Bb	C	D	Eb	F	G	Ab	Bb
E	E	F#	G#	A	B	C#	D#	E	F#	G#	A	B
F	F	G	A	Bb	C	D	E	F	G	A	Bb	C
F#	F#	G#	A#	B	C#	D#	E#	F#	G#	A#	B	C#
Gb	Gb	Ab	Bb	Cb	Db	Eb	F	Gb	Ab	Bb	Cb	Db
G	G	A	B	C	D	E	F#	G	A	B	C	D
Ab	Ab	Bb	C	Db	Eb	F	G	Ab	Bb	C	Db	Eb
A	A	B	C#	D	E	F#	G#	A	B	C#	D	E
Bb	Bb	C	D	Eb	F	G	A	Bb	C	D	Eb	F
B	B	C#	D#	E	F#	G#	A#	B	C#	D#	E	F#

F# and Gb major scales are enharmonic, as are the C# and Db Dominant scales.

Intervals

We have seen that scales can be expressed in three ways, as notes, as scale degrees, and as a step-pattern. There is also a fourth way: **Intervals**.

Understanding intervals is basic to understanding melody, harmony and the structure of chords. The concept of intervals underlies all of music theory. We are already familiar with scale degrees.

Scale Degrees:	1	2	3	4	5	6	7
Scale of Notes (in C):	C	D	E	F	G	A	B

Intervals describe the distances between notes.

Scale Degree:	1	2	3	4	5	6	7	8	
Step-pattern:		w	w	h	w	w	w	h	
C Major scale:	C	D	E	F	G	A	B	C	
	1	2							Two Semitones
	Second								
	1	2	3						Four Semitones
	Third								
	1	2	3	4					Five Semitones
	Fourth								
Interval:	1	2	3	4	5				Seven Semitones
(Distance)	Fifth								
	1	2	3	4	5	6			Nine Semitones
	Sixth								
	1	2	3	4	5	6	7		Eleven Semitones
	Seventh								
	1	2	3	4	5	6	7	8	Twelve Semitones
	Octave								

Intervals are counted in tones and semitones. One whole tone = two semitones. For example, to go from C to D is one whole tone or two semitones. With Intervals, the starting note is counted as 1, so to go from C (1) to D (2) is the interval of a second. If we go from C to E, we are going up three notes (counting C as 1) from C (1) to D (2) to E (3), so from C to E is the interval of a third.

An interval is the distance between two notes, any two notes – it doesn't have to start on the root. In the C scale, the distance between C and G is a fifth because the G is the fifth degree of the scale, five notes up from C (counting C as 1). The distance from E to B is also an interval of a fifth because B is five notes up from E (counting E as 1).

Scale Degree:	1	2	3	4	5	6	7
C Scale:	C	D	E	F	G	A	B
Intervals:			1	2	3	4	5
			Interval of a Fifth				
	1	2	3	4	5		
	Interval of a Fifth						

Intervals of more than one octave are called **Compound Intervals**; for example, from C to the D above octave C is a 9th; from C to the F above octave C is an 11th; from C to the A above octave C is a 13th.

Scale Degree:	1	2	3	4	5	6	7	8	9	10	11	12	13
C Major scale:	C	D	E	F	G	A	B	C	D	E	F	G	A
Intervals:	1	2	3	4	5	6	7	8	9				
	Ninth												
	1	2	3	4	5	6	7	8	9	10	11		
	Eleventh												
	1	2	3	4	5	6	7	8	9	10	11	12	13
	Thirteenth												

Musical intervals result in some interesting math:

Scale Degree:	1	2	3	4	5	6	7
C Scale:	C	D	E	F	G	A	B
Intervals:	Third						
			Third				
	Fifth						

In the C scale, the interval between the C and the G is a fifth. But the interval between the C and E is a third and the interval between the E and the G is a third, which is two thirds: shouldn't that make a sixth? But C to G is a fifth, so in music does 3+3 = 5?

No. C to G is a fifth. Although we have two thirds, in each third the starting note is counted as one, so the E is in there twice, as the third note of the first third and the first note of the second third. So although we are counting three tones from C to E and three tones from E to G, we are counting a total of five tones from C to G.

Intervals are integral to music and there is a lot of theory about them; they can be major, minor, pure, perfect, augmented, diminished, vertical, horizontal, linear, harmonic, melodic, stable, unstable, consonant and dissonant. Intervals are important because the tuning of instruments depends on intervals; the bass is tuned in fourths. Intervals are noted in mathematical ratios called the Harmonic Series for example,

- an octave is 2:1, twice the frequency of the tonic
- a Perfect Fifth is 3:2
- a Perfect Fourth is 4:3
- a major third is 5:4
- a minor third is 6:5

The problem with the mathematical intervals of the Harmonic Series is that stacking pure fifths will eventually result in a dissonance, called the Wolf Interval, a problem for early tuning systems such as just intonation and quarter comma meantone temperament. There were even enharmonic keyboards invented with split keys for the same notes in different pitches to be played in different keys.

Today we use Equal Temperament (dividing the chromatic scale into twelve equal semitones), which slightly diminishes the fifths so that melodies can be transposed to different keys without dissonance.

Major and Minor Intervals

Intervals can be major, minor or perfect. Let's look at the interval of a third:

C	C#/D♭	D	D#/E♭	E	F	G	A	B	C
2 semitones									
Whole Tone									
		2 semitones							
		Whole Tone							
4 semitones									
2 Whole Tones									
Major Third									

Although we have three notes, C-D-E, we have four semitones, C to D♭ - D♭ to D - D to E♭ - E♭ to E. Four semitones equals two whole tones. This is called a **Major Third**.

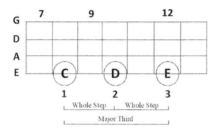

Intervals don't have to start on the root, we can count up three tones starting anywhere in the scale:

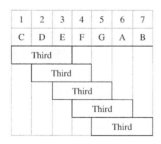

1	2	3	4	5	6	7
C	D	E	F	G	A	B
Third						
	Third					
		Third				
			Third			
				Third		

But all these thirds are not equal:

Diatonic Scale Degree:	1		2		3	4		5		6		7
Chromatic Scale:	C	C#/Db	D	D#/Eb	E	F	F#/Gb	G	G#/Ab	A	A#/Bb	B

Intervals:
- C to E — Third — 4 Semitones
- D to F — Third — 3 Semitones
- E to G — Third — 3 Semitones
- F to A — Third — 4 Semitones
- G to B — Third — 4 Semitones

From C to E we have four semitones, but from D to F, we have only three semitones because of the natural half-step between E/F. From D to E is a whole tone, or two semitones, from E to F is only a semitone, making three semitones total. A third with four semitones is called a **Major Third**; a third with three semitones is called a **Minor Third**.

Diatonic Scale Degree:	1		2		3	4		5		6		7
Chromatic Scale:	C	C#/Db	D	D#/Eb	E	F	F#/Gb	G	G#/Ab	A	A#/Bb	B
4 Semitones		Major Third										
3 Semitones				Minor Third								
3 Semitones						Minor Third						
4 Semitones							Major Third					
4 Semitones									Major Third			

Our major scale thus naturally contains both major and minor thirds.

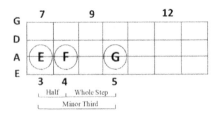

A major third can be turned into a minor third by making one of the notes flat.

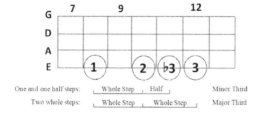

One and one half steps:	Whole Step	Half	Minor Third
Two whole steps:	Whole Step	Whole Step	Major Third

Besides major and minor thirds, we can have major and minor 6th and major and minor 7th.

C Scale:	C	D	Eb	E	F	G	Ab	A	Bb	B	C
Scale Degree:	1	2	b3	3	4	5	b6	6	b7	7	8
3 Semitones	Minor 3rd										
4 Semitones	Major 3rd										
8 Semitones	Minor 6th										
9 Semitones	Major 6th										
10 Semitones	Minor 7th										
11 Semitones	Major 7th										

Minor intervals give us our minor scale. Compared to the major scale, the minor scale has a flat 3rd, flat 6th and flat 7th.

- In the Major Scale, the 2nd, 3rd, 6th and 7th are Major Intervals.
- In the Minor Scale, the 3rd, 6th and 7th are Minor Intervals.
- In both the major and minor scales, the 4th and 5th are Perfect, neither major nor minor.
- The Unison, or Prime or Tonic, and the Octave are also Perfect.

The degree of an interval is called its Quantity, for example, third, seventh, etc. Whether it is major, minor or perfect is called its Quality. Intervals can also be harmonic or melodic. Harmonic means that the notes are played together, as in a chord; melodic means that they are played separately, one note at a time, as in an arpeggio or bassline.

Here is a table of the major and minor scale intervals:

		Octave							
		Major 7th							
		Major 6th							
Major Scale Intervals		Perfect 5th							
		Perfect 4th							
		Major 3rd							
		Major 2nd							
Major Scale Degree		1	2	3	4	5	6	7	8
C Major Scale		C	D	E	F	G	A	B	C
Cm Scale		C	D	E♭	F	G	A♭	B♭	C
Minor Scale Degree		1	2	♭3	4	5	♭6	♭7	8
		Major 2nd							
		Minor 3rd							
		Perfect 4th							
Minor Scale Intervals		Perfect 5th							
		Minor 6th							
		Minor 7th							
		Octave							

The natural half-steps in the diatonic scale affect the counting of intervals. The interval of a fourth, C-D-E-F, contains the natural half-step of E/F, resulting in five semitones, but it is not a minor fourth, it is called a Perfect Fourth. When we count in thirds, the natural half-step between E/F is counted as a semitone, giving us three semitones from D to F, a minor third.

Diatonic Scale Degree:	1		2		3	4		5		6		7
Semitones:	0	1	2	3	4	5	6	7	8	9	10	11
Chromatic Scale:	C	C#/D♭	D	D#/E♭	E	F	F#/G♭	G	G#/A♭	A	A#/B♭	B
4 Semitones		Major Third										
3 Semitones			Minor Third									
5 Semitones		Perfect Fourth										

Augmented and Diminished Intervals

Intervals can be major or minor; they can also be augmented or diminished.

A minor interval has one semitone less than a major interval; for example, a minor third has three semitones, one less than a major third which has four semitones.

Scale Degrees:	1		2		3	4		5		6		7	8
Semitones:	0	1	2	3	4	5	6	7	8	9	10	11	12
Chromatic Scale:	C	Db	D	Eb	E	F	F#/Gb	G	G#/Ab	A	Bb	B	C
3 Semitones			Minor 3rd										
4 Semitones			Major 3rd										

An Augmented interval has one more semitone than a major or a perfect interval; for example, an augmented fourth has six semitones, one more than the five semitones of a perfect fourth.

Scale Degrees:	1		2		3	4		5		6		7	8
Semitones:	0	1	2	3	4	5	6	7	8	9	10	11	12
Chromatic Scale:	C	C#/Db	D	D#/Eb	E	F	F#	G	G#/Ab	A	A#/Bb	B	C
5 Semitones			Perfect 4th										
6 Semitones			Augmented 4th										

A Diminished interval has one less semitone than a minor interval; it's like a double minor. For example, E-F-G is a minor third with three semitones (one semitone between E/F and two semitones between F/G for a total of three semitones). If we reduce the G by a semitone to Gb, we have two semitones from E to Gb. Two semitones is a diminished third. When we have a fifth and reduce it by a half-step, it is called a diminished fifth rather than a minor fifth, because with the half-step between E/F, the interval of E-F-G is a minor third, so taking it down another half-step to E-F-Gb is like a double minor, which is called diminished.

Scale Degrees:	1		2		3	4		5		6		7	8
Semitones:	0	1	2	3	4	5	6	7	8	9	10	11	12
Chromatic Scale:	C	C#/Db	D	D#/Eb	E	F	Gb	G	G#/Ab	A	A#/Bb	B	C
3 Semitones					Minor 3rd								
2 Semitones					Dim 3rd								
6 Semitones			Diminished 5th										
7 Semitones			Perfect 5th										

Perfect Fourth and Perfect Fifth

The fourth and fifth intervals, along with the tonic and octave, are called Perfect. The history of this goes back to the 6th century BC with Pythagorean ideas of harmony and the Perfect ratios of the octave, 2:1; the fifth, 3:2; and the fourth, 4:3. In modern usage, Perfect means that the fourth and fifth have no major or minor function, that is, they are the same in the major and minor scales, unlike the third, sixth and seventh.

Major Scale Degree:	1	2	3	4	5	6	7	8
Major Scale Step-pattern:		w	w	h	w	w	w	h
C Major Scale:	C	D	E	F	G	A	B	C
Cm Scale:	C	D	E♭	F	G	A♭	B♭	C
Minor Scale Step-pattern:		w	h	w	w	h	w	w
Minor Scale Degree:	1	2	♭3	4	5	♭6	♭7	8

You may notice that besides the 4th and 5th, the 2nd doesn't change between the major and minor scales, so why isn't it called a Perfect Second? It's because a second can be made minor, ♭2, but the 4th and 5th can't be made minor, they can only be made diminished.

The Perfect Fourth and Perfect Fifth are reciprocal inversions of each other. Raising a fifth above the tonic is the same as descending a fourth from the octave.

Major Scale Degree:	1	2	3	4	5	6	7	8
C Major Scale:	C	D	E	F	G	A	B	C
Ascending:	Fifth →							
Descending:					← Fourth			
Scale Degree:	8	7	6	5	4	3	2	1

We can see this on the bass fretboard. In the key of D, the fifth is A, which occurs in two octave positions relative to the tonic:

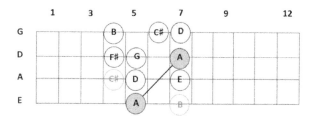

If we count up 5 from the tonic, we reach the 5th:

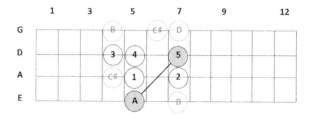

But counting down from the tonic, we count down four notes to the octave 5th:

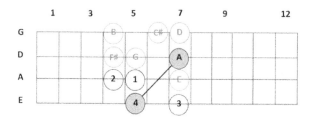

Similarly, raising by a 4th is the same as lowering by a 5th:

Major Scale Degree:	1	2	3	4	5	6	7	8
C Major Scale:	C	D	E	F	G	A	B	C
Ascending:				Fourth →				
Descending:					← Fifth			
Scale Degree:	8	7	6	5	4	3	2	1

Tritone

An interval of three whole tones is called a **Tritone**. In the major diatonic scale, there is only one natural tritone of three whole tones, F-G-A-B with F to G being one whole tone, G to A a second whole tone and A to B a third whole tone, making three consecutive whole tones.

Scale Degree:	1	2	3	4	5	6	7	8
C Major Scale:	C	D	E	F	G	A	B	C
Step-pattern:		w	w	h	w	w	w	h

In the recurring step-pattern, wherever three whole tones occur in a series, that's a tritone.

···w-w-h-**w-w-w**-h-w-w-h-**w-w-w**-h-w-w-h-**w-w-w**-h-w-w-h···:‖ Repeat

Three consecutive whole tones will only occur once in any given scale.

Three whole tones equals six semitones. If we say a tritone is any six semitones, then the Augmented 4th/Diminished 5th is a tritone, the infamous ♭5 of the Devil's Tritone found in the Locrian mode.

The ♭5 occurs exactly in the middle of the scale, 6 semitones from the Tonic and 6 semitones from the Octave.

Scale Degrees:	1	♭2	2	♭3	3	4	♭5	5	♭6	6	♭7	7	8
Semitones:	0	1	2	3	4	5	6	7	8	9	10	11	12
Chromatic Scale:	C (Dbb)	C# Db	D (Ebb)	D# Eb	E (Fb)	F (E#)	F# Gb	G (Abb)	G# Ab	A (Bbb)	A# Bb	B (Cb)	C (B#)
6 Semitones		Augmented 4th											
		Diminished 5th											

Another place tritones occur is when two minor thirds are together. A minor third is 3 semitones, so two minor thirds is 6 semitones which is a tritone.

In harmony, tritones are known as unstable intervals that sound discordant and so strongly seek resolution to a consonant chord.

Interval Chart

Scale Degrees	1		2		3	4		5		6		7	8
Semitones:	0	1	2	3	4	5	6	7	8	9	10	11	12
Chromatic Scale:	C (Dbb)	C# Db	D (Ebb)	D# Eb	E (Fb)	F (E#)	F# Gb	G (Abb)	G# Ab	A (Bbb)	A# Bb	B (Cb)	C (B#)

0 Semitones	Prime / Dim 2
1 Semitone	Aug Prime / Minor 2nd
2 Semitones	Major 2nd / Diminished 3rd
3 Semitones	Augmented 2nd / Minor 3rd
4 Semitones	Major 3rd / Diminished 4th
5 Semitones	Augmented 3rd / Perfect 4th
6 Semitones	Augmented 4th / Diminished 5th
7 Semitones	Perfect 5th / Diminished 6th
8 Semitones	Augmented 5th / Minor 6th
9 Semitones	Major 6th / Diminished 7th
10 Semitones	Augmented 6th / Minor 7th
11 Semitones	Major 7th / Diminished Octave
12 Semitones	Augmented 7th / Perfect Octave

With intervals, the tonic is called the Unison (or Perfect Unison or Prime or Perfect Prime) and the octave is called the Perfect Octave. (Any two notes of multiples of the same pitch played together can be called a Unison, such as playing C_2 and the octave C_3 together, but it is often used for the first tone of the scale.)

It may seem that intervals with two names and the same number of semitones are equivalent, but musically they have different functions. An augmented 4th is used differently than a diminished 5th even though they both have 6 semitones.

Of the twenty-six intervals, the most common are:

- minor third
- major third
- perfect fourth
- diminished fifth
- perfect fifth
- augmented fifth
- minor sixth
- major sixth
- minor seventh
- major seventh
- octave

The minor third and minor seventh intervals may also informally be called flat third or flat seventh, although minor refers to the interval and flat refers to the scale degree.

Consonance and Dissonance

The harmonic relationship of intervals is called consonance and dissonance – consonance means they sound complete together, dissonance means they sound incomplete. The ear is always listening for a return to the stable home-tone of the tonic, from dissonance to harmony. This is called resolution.

Some intervals are consonant and some are dissonant. The most common dissonant interval used in chords is the ♭7. Adding the dissonant flat seven to a major chord pushes for movement from dissonance to consonance. You will sometimes hear a major chord played at the end of a verse changed to a 7th chord to prepare the ear for a movement to the chorus.

There is a whole complex field of harmonic theory to explain consonance and dissonance.

Interval:	Note:				
Unison	C	1	Perfect Consonance	0 Semitones	Tonic
Minor 2nd	D♭	♭2	*Dissonant*	1 Semitone	Supertonic
Major 2nd	D	2	*Dissonant*	2 Semitones	Supertonic
Minor 3rd	E♭	♭3	Imperfect Consonance	3 Semitones	Mediant
Major 3rd	E	3	Imperfect Consonance	4 Semitones	Mediant
Perfect 4th	F	4	Perfect Consonance	5 Semitones	Subdominant
Diminished 5th	G♭	♭5	*Dissonant*	6 Semitones	Tritone
Perfect 5th	G	5	Perfect Consonance	7 Semitones	Dominant
Minor 6th	A♭	♭6	Imperfect Consonance	8 Semitones	Sub-Mediant
Major 6th	A	6	Imperfect Consonance	9 Semitones	Sub-Mediant
Minor 7th	B♭	♭7	*Dissonant*	10 Semitones	Subtonic
Major 7th	B	7	*Dissonant*	11 Semitones	Leading Tone
Octave	C	8	Perfect Consonance	12 Semitones	Octave

The Leading Tone, or seventh degree of the major scale, is a half-step below the tonic. The ♭7 is a whole tone (two semitones) below the tonic and is called the Subtonic.

The dissonant intervals of 2nd and 7th are equivalent, or reciprocal, because if you count up from the tonic you have a second, but if you count down from the octave, you have a seventh.

Major Scale Degree:	1	2	3	4	5	6	7	8
C Major Scale:	C	D	E	F	G	A	B	C
Ascending:	$2^{nd} \rightarrow$							
Descending:					$\leftarrow 7^{th}$			
Scale Degree:	8	7	6	5	4	3	2	1

Rising a minor second (2 semitones) from the tonic is the same as descending a major 7th (11 semitones) from the octave; rising a major second (2 semitones) is the same as descending a minor 7th (10 semitones). Similarly, descending a second is the same as rising a 7th.

The table of consonant and dissonant intervals gives us three groups:

Interval:	Note:			
Minor 2nd	D♭	♭2	Dissonant	1 Semitone
Major 2nd	D	2	Dissonant	2 Semitones
Diminished 5th	G♭	♭5	Dissonant	6 Semitones
Minor 7th	B♭	♭7	Dissonant	10 Semitones
Major 7th	B	7	Dissonant	11 Semitones
Minor 3rd	E♭	♭3	Imperfect Consonance	3 Semitones
Major 3rd	E	3	Imperfect Consonance	4 Semitones
Minor 6th	A♭	♭6	Imperfect Consonance	8 Semitones
Major 6th	A	6	Imperfect Consonance	9 Semitones
Unison	C	1	Perfect Consonance	0 Semitones
Perfect 4th	F	4	Perfect Consonance	5 Semitones
Perfect 5th	G	5	Perfect Consonance	7 Semitones
Octave	C	8	Perfect Consonance	12 Semitones

Harmony

Melodic harmony depends on a balance of consonance and dissonance. Harmony is the human part of music theory because it has to do more with the feeling and emotion of a melody than the mathematical ratios of the Harmonic Series. But there are certain principles governing the relationships of tones we perceive as consonant or dissonant. The principles of harmony come from Pythagoras through the Medieval church modes, through Renaissance counterpoint and into chordal accompaniment key-centered composition.

There are four ways a harmony line, like a bassline, can move in relation to the melody:

- *Similar Motion* – both lines move in the same direction – for example, the melody line moves up a third and the bassline moves up a sixth.
- *Parallel Motion* – both lines move in the same direction by the same amount – for example, the melody line moves up a third and the bass line moves up a third as well.
- *Contrary Motion* – the lines move in opposite directions – for example, the melody moves up a third and the bass moves down a fifth.
- *Oblique Motion* – one line moves while the other stays the same – for example, the melody moves up a third while the bass remains on the tonic.

Too much Similar and Parallel motion can make for a bland accompaniment, so they need to be broken up with Contrary and Oblique motion to add interest and depth. Harmony typically targets the Imperfect Consonances of the 3rd and 6th interspersed with dissonant and perfect consonances. Going down a third is reciprocal to going up a sixth.

Major Scale Degree:	1	2	3	4	5	6	7	8
C Major Scale:	C	D	E	F	G	A	B	C
Ascending:			$3^{rd} \rightarrow$					
Descending:				$\leftarrow 6^{th}$				
Scale Degree:	8	7	6	5	4	3	2	1

Rising a major 3rd from the tonic is the same as descending a minor 6th from the octave. Rising a minor 3rd is the same as descending a major 6th. Similarly, descending a third is the same as rising a 6th.

71

The important thing to take away here is that harmony is locked into the intervals.

Harmony depends on the relationship of notes in the scale to the tonic, called tonality. Generally, flat notes have gravity and want to move down, giving a darker tone, while sharp notes want to move up, giving a brighter, more uplifting tone, as we can hear in the difference between major and minor keys. The sharp keys of G, D, A and E are more common in popular music than the flat keys of F, B♭, E♭ and A♭.

All the whole tones of the scale want to resolve downwards, the fourth wants to move down to the third rather than up to the fifth; the sixth wants to move down to the fifth. The exception is the 7th, the leading tone, which wants to resolve upwards to the octave. These note movements are only tendencies as notes can move up or down as determined by the melody; although the fourth tends to move down to the third, it can also move up to the fifth.

Intervals are classed as stable and unstable. Stable means they feel like a resting place. The more unstable the tone, the more it wants to move somewhere. In melody this usually means that stable notes can be held longer than unstable notes; the more unstable the note, the shorter its duration.

The most stable intervals in the scale are the 1st-3rd-5th, which are the basic tones of a chord. The third is the most independent of the tonic and whether the third is flat or not defines whether the scale is major or minor. The fifth is not as stable as the third having a stronger feeling of wanting to return to the tonic, the most stable home tone.

Next in stability are the intervals of the 2nd and 6th. These, along with the 1-3-5 chord tones, make up the major pentatonic scale, 1-2-3-5-6.

Less stable than the pentatonic notes are the 4th, 7th and ♭7th. These are transitional, moving tones

Even less stable are the ♭3 and ♭5. The ♭3 of the minor scale is disturbing and makes us want to relieve the distress by returning to the safety and stability of the tonic. The ♭5, used in diminished chords and the blues scale, is called a Blue Note because its minor tonality is so dark, dangerous and bluesy – it's the ♭5 of the Devil's Tritone.

Least stable of all are the ♭2 and ♭6, which are typically only used as passing tones.

Knowing this is important for basslines as we don't want to dwell on the unstable tones, but use them as stepping stones to the stable tones.

Chords

When three or more notes are played together, it is called a Chord (although there are two note chords). Notes can be added and subtracted from chords resulting in many variations. Chords can be major, minor, seventh, major seventh, augmented, diminished, suspended, added, etc.

But all these variations depend on three notes, called a **triad**. The basic notes of a major chord are the first, third and fifth notes of the scale. In C that is C-E-G making a C major chord.

When talking scales, the first note is called the tonic, but when talking chords, the first note is called the **Root**. The Root note determines the name of the chord: if the root note is C, then it is in the family of C chords, if an Eb then it is in the Eb family of chords, etc.

As an interesting aside, you may wonder how a three-note chord is played on a six-string guitar. Well, the position of the fingers adjusts the strings to the chord tones. Here is a C chord played on guitar:

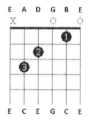

The names of the open strings are shown across the top and the actual notes played are shown along the bottom. As you can see, although there are six strings, only three notes are played, C-E-G, the notes of the C major chord.

Major Chords

A chord is a group of notes played together. A basic chord is made up of three notes, called a triad. A chord triad consists of the root, the third and the fifth note of the scale. In the key of C, the notes of the C chord are C, E and G. Chords using the 1-3-5 intervals of the major scale are called **Major Chords**.

Scale Degree:	1	2	3	4	5	6	7	1-3-5	
C Scale:	C	D	E	F	G	A	B	C-E-G	C Major chord

The pitches of the chord are called **chord tones** and playing a chord one note at a time is an **arpeggio**. Other notes in the scale, but not in the major chord, the 2, 4 and 6 scale degrees, are called **non-chord tones**. The 7th is a special case, often played flat in 7th chords.

In some songs a bass player can get away with playing only the root, or the root and the fifth – very common in folk and country music. When just the root is played repeatedly, it is called a **Pedal**.

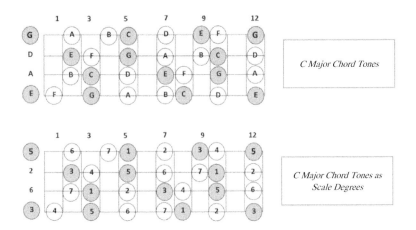

C Major Chord Tones

C Major Chord Tones as Scale Degrees

There are many variations of the basic chord tones. The 3rd can be flat, making a minor chord. The 5th note can be either sharp or flat, giving us an augmented or diminished chord. The seventh note can be flat, making a dominant 7th chord. Other variations of the notes give us suspended chords, slash chords, power chords, added tone chords and so on, but they are all variations of that basic 1-3-5 chord structure.

Minor Chords

Minor Chords are built on the minor scale. Minor chords use the same triad as major chords only with a minor, or flatted, third. The minor triad is 1-♭3-5.

Scale Degree:	1	2	♭3	4	5	♭6	♭7	1-♭3-5	
C Minor Scale:	C	D	E♭	F	G	A♭	B♭	C-E♭-G	C minor chord

The C major chord is C-E-G. The Cm chord is C-E♭-G. That's the only difference between a Major and a Minor chord, that one note, the flat third. This is extremely important for playing bass as the third determines whether you are playing a major or minor chord.

Major Scale Degree:	1	2	3	4	5	6	7	8		
Major Scale Step-pattern:		w	w	h	w	w	w	h		
C Major Scale:	C	D	E	F	G	A	B	C	C-E-G	C Major
Cm Scale:	C	D	E♭	F	G	A♭	B♭	C	C-E♭-G	C minor
Minor Scale Step-pattern:		w	h	w	w	h	w	w		
Minor Scale Degree:	1	2	♭3	4	5	♭6	♭7	8		

Notice that the fifth is the same note in both C major and Cm. The fifth is Perfect and has neither major nor minor function. This means that roots and fifths can be played over both major and minor chords.

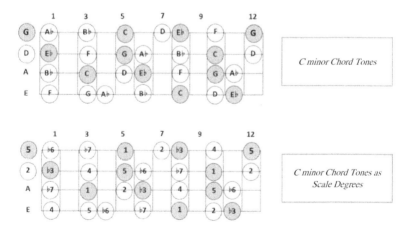

C minor Chord Tones

C minor Chord Tones as Scale Degrees

Chord Structure – Stacked Thirds

The C major chord is the 1-3-5 of the scale, giving us C-E-G. This 1-3-5 structure is made up of two thirds. This is called **stacked thirds**, or Tertian Harmony.

Scale Degree:	1	2	3	4	5	6	7
C Major Scale:	C	D	E	F	G	A	B
Stacked Thirds:	Third						
			Third				

If we look a little more closely at the thirds of the chords we will see that the first third in the C major chord is a major third, two whole steps, C-D-E. However, the following third, from E to G, E-F-G, is only one and a half steps because of the natural half-step between the E and the F – which gives us a minor third. So, the C major chord is made up of both a major third and a minor third – a minor third stacked on a major third.

Scale Degree:	1	2	3	4	5	6	7	8
C Major Scale:	C	D	E	F	G	A	B	C
Intervals:		w	w	h	w	w	w	h
Stacked Thirds:	Major Third							
			Minor Third					

Minor chords are also built from stacked thirds.

Scale Degree:	1	2	♭3	4	5	♭6	♭7
C minor Scale:	C	D	E♭	F	G	A♭	B♭
Stacked Thirds:	Third						
			Third				

With the C minor chord we have a minor third, C-D-E♭, 1-2-♭3, one and a half steps from the root, and a major third, E♭-F-G, ♭3-4-5, two full steps. This gives us the C minor chord C-E♭-G; the 1-♭3-5 of the minor scale.

Scale Degree:	1	2	♭3	4	5	♭6	♭7	8
C Minor Scale:	C	D	E♭	F	G	A♭	B♭	C
Intervals:		w	h	w	w	h	w	w
Stacked Thirds:	Minor Third							
		Major Third						

The C minor chord is made up of both a minor third and a major third – a major third stacked on a minor third.

Both the major and minor chords are made up of a major and a minor third. When we have a major third followed by a minor third, we call it a major chord. When we have a minor third followed by a major third, we call it a minor chord.

Chords take their quality from the first third – if the first third is major, then it is a major chord; if the first third is minor, then it is a minor chord.

Major Seventh Chords

Major Seventh Chords are formed by adding the 7th note of the scale to a major chord triad.

In C, the 1-3-5 triad, C-E-G, gives us the C major chord. If we go up another third from G, two more whole steps, G-A-B, we add the 7th note of the scale, in this case B, which gives us 1-3-5-7, C-E-G-B, a Major 7th chord.

Scale Degree:	1	2	3	4	5	6	7	1-3-5-7	
C Major Scale:	C	D	E	F	G	A	B	C-E-G-B	CMaj7 chord
		w	w	h	w	w	w		
		Major Third							
Stacked Thirds:			Minor Third						
				Major Third					
		Major 7th							

A major third followed by a minor third followed by another major third gives us a major 7 chord. Note that the 'major' refers to the Major 7th interval and not to the major chord – it's C (major 7th), not (C major) 7th.

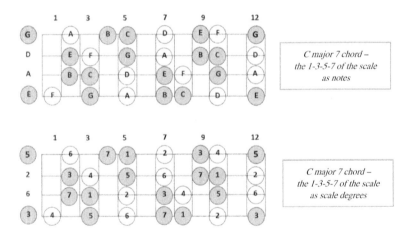

C major 7 chord –
the 1-3-5-7 of the scale
as notes

C major 7 chord –
the 1-3-5-7 of the scale
as scale degrees

Major 7th chords are written CMaj7, Cmaj7, CM7, CΔ7 or CΔ.

Seventh Chords

A **Seventh Chord**, or **Dominant Seventh Chord**, is formed when a flat 7 is added to a major chord.

There is a section following about **Dominant Seventh Chords** that will explain the proper theory behind 7th chords, but for now we will treat 7th chords as if they were built on stacked intervals of a third of the notes of the scale.

With the major 7th chord, we stacked a major third onto the major chord, but we can stack a minor third onto the major chord instead, G-A-Bb, with one and a half steps between the G and the Bb. This adds the flat or minor 7, making the chord C-E-G-Bb; 1-3-5-b7, a 7th chord.

Scale Degree:	1	2	3	4	5	6	b7	1-3-5-b7	
C Dominant Scale:	C	D	E	F	G	A	Bb	C-E-G-Bb	C7 chord
		w	w	h	w	w	h		
		Major Third							
Stacked Thirds:			Minor Third						
				Minor Third					
			Minor 7th						

A major third followed by two minor thirds gives us a 7th chord. The chord with the flat 7 is properly called a dominant 7th chord, but is usually just called a 7th chord. The 7th chord is the most common chord extension. (A chord extension is any note added to the basic triad.)

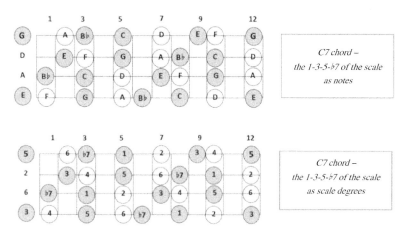

C7 chord –
the 1-3-5-b7 of the scale
as notes

C7 chord –
the 1-3-5-b7 of the scale
as scale degrees

The difference between Major 7th chords and 7th chords is that the Major 7th chord uses the natural scale tone of the major 7 note, 1-3-5-7. The 7th chord uses the flatted 7 note of the scale, 1-3-5-♭7. They are both extensions of major chords with the major 7th stacking a major third onto the chord and the dominant 7th stacking a minor third; or the major 7th using a major 7th interval and the dominant 7th using a minor 7th interval.

Major 7 chords are usually designated as CMaj7 or Cmaj7 or sometimes CM7, whereas 7th chords are written simply as C7. Whenever you see a 7 added to a chord, you know that it has an added flat seven: D7 is a D major chord with an added C, the flat 7 of the D scale; G7 is a G major chord with an added F, the flat 7 of the G scale.

Seventh chords very strongly want to resolve to a consonant chord. This is because all dominant 7th chords have an unstable tritone of six semitones: from degree 3 to 5 is three semitones and from 5 to ♭7 is three semitones, two stacked minor thirds.

Minor Seventh Chords

A **Minor 7ᵗʰ Chord** is a minor chord with the added flat 7: 1-♭3-5-♭7. In Cm we have C-E♭-G-B♭; usually noted as Cm7.

The minor 7ᵗʰ chord is created by adding a minor third to the minor chord triad.

Scale Degree:	1	2	♭3	4	5	♭6	♭7	1-♭3-5-♭7	
C minor Scale:	C	D	E♭	F	G	A♭	B♭	C-E♭-G-B♭	Cm7 chord
Intervals:		w	h	w	w	h	w		
Stacked Thirds:		Minor Third							
			Major Third						
					Minor Third				
		Minor 7ᵗʰ							

A minor third followed by a major third followed by another minor third gives us the minor 7ᵗʰ chord.

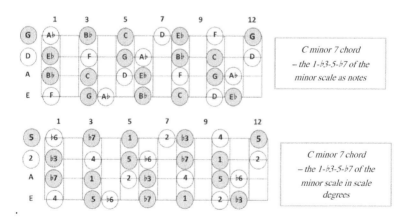

C minor 7 chord
– the 1-♭3-5-♭7 of the minor scale as notes

C minor 7 chord
– the 1-♭3-5-♭7 of the minor scale in scale degrees

With major 7 chords we saw that the 'major' referred to the 7 and not the chord; for example, a Cmaj7 is a C major chord with an added major seventh. The major refers to the 7, not to the chord. It's C (major 7), not (C major) 7. However, with a minor 7ᵗʰ chord, the 'minor' refers to the chord, not the 7; for example, a Cm7 is a minor chord with an added ♭7. It's (C minor) 7, not C (minor 7).

Stacking major and minor thirds in different combinations gives us different kinds of chords.

- The thirds of a C7 chord are stacked:
  Major Third–Minor Third–Minor Third.
- The thirds of a Cm7 are stacked:
  Minor Third–Major Third–Minor Third.

Both the major and minor 7th chords have one Major Third and two Minor Thirds, but in a different order.

Minor Major Seventh Chords

Besides the minor 7th chord there is also a minor major 7th chord that adds the major 7th note of the scale instead of the flat 7, 1-♭3-5-7; that is, adding a major third to the minor chord. The corresponding scale is the harmonic minor scale, a minor scale with a major 7 note. The minor major 7th in C would be written as CmMaj7.

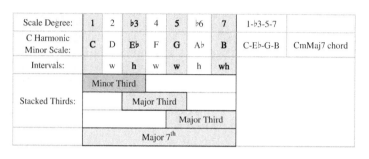

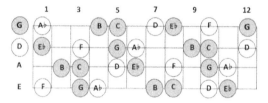

C minor 7 Major chord – the 1-♭3-5-7 of the minor scale as notes

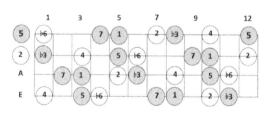

C minor Major 7 chord – the 1-♭3-5-7 of the minor scale in scale degrees

83

Dominant 7th Chords

In the chapter on **Seventh Chords**, seventh chords were presented as made up of a chord, such as the C major chord of C-E-G, with an added flat 7, giving us the C7 chord of C-E-G-B♭, stacking a minor third onto the major chord triad. In scale degrees, that would be the 1-3-5-♭7 of the scale. Most people learn 7th chords as extensions of major and minor chords, stacking a minor third on top of the chord triad. This is a practical explanation, but isn't quite correct according to harmonic theory. In harmonic theory, the C7 chord is actually derived from the F scale, not the C scale.

The explanation about Dominant 7th chords is the kind of thing that turns people off from music theory. It seems like an abstruse and overly complicated explanation of something quite simple. But it is really an example of how everything in music is interconnected. It shows some of the inner workings of music. When you push down on the accelerator in a car, it goes forward; pretty simple, right? But what you don't see is the interconnected system of linkages and gears and electrical signals all working together to move the car. So the theory behind Dominant 7th chords isn't useless nonsense, it's a peek under the hood.

The seventh chord is awkward because the flat 7th note of the C7 chord, B♭, is not in the C major diatonic scale, C-D-E-F-G-A-B-C, it is a chromatic note falling in between A and B:

Scale Degree:	1	2	3	4	5	6	♭7	7	8
C major scale:	C	D	E	F	G	A	**B♭**	B	C

But we can derive the seventh chord from a related Dominant scale. The Dominant scale begins on the 5th of the root scale and uses the same notes as the root scale. For example, in the F major scale, the 5th note is C, so we can start a scale on C:

Scale Degree:	1	2	3	4	5	6	7	8/1	2	3	4	5	6
F Major Scale:	F	G	A	B♭	C	D	E	F	G	A	B♭	C	D
C Dominant Scale:					C	D	E	F	G	A	B♭	C	
Scale Degree:					1	2	3	4	5	6	♭7	8/1	

84

Notice that the F scale has a naturally occurring B♭ in the 4th scale degree, F-G-A-B♭-C-D-E, and so the C Dominant scale derived from F also has a B♭, but in the 7th scale degree. If we build a chord by stacking thirds of the C dominant scale we get:

Scale Degree:	1	2	3	4	5	6	♭7	8/1	1-3-5-♭7	
C Dominant Scale:	C	D	E	F	G	A	B♭	C	C-E-G-B♭	C7 chord

This is why 7th chords are called Dominant 7th chords, because they are derived from a scale starting on the Dominant, or fifth, of a scale. The C Dominant scale has a natural B♭ at the 7th scale degree, which is why 7th chords are written with a plain 7 (C7) instead of ♭7 (C♭7), because in the Dominant scale, the 7 is not flat, it is a natural half-step note. However, when compared to the C major scale, the C dominant scale can be said to have a ♭7.

Scale Degree:	1	2	3	4	5	6	7	8/1	1-3-5-7	
C Major Scale:	C	D	E	F	G	A	B	C	C-E-G-B	CMaj7 chord
C Dominant Scale:	C	D	E	F	G	A	B♭	C	C-E-G-B♭	C7 chord
Scale Degree:	1	2	3	4	5	6	♭7	8/1	1-3-5-♭7	

The added tone chords of 9th, 11th and 13th are also built on the Dominant scale as they include the ♭7.

Here are the Dominant scales and the 7th chords derived from them:

Root Scale:	5/1	2	3	4	5	6	b7	8	1-3-5-b7	Chord:
				Dominant Scales						
C	G	A	B	C	D	E	F	G	G-B-D-F	G7
Db	Ab	Bb	C	Db	Eb	F	Gb	Ab	Ab-C-Eb-Gb	Ab7
D	A	B	C#	D	E	F#	G	A	A-C#-E-G	A7
Eb	Bb	C	D	Eb	F	G	Ab	Bb	Bb-D-F-Ab	Bb7
E	B	C#	D#	E	F#	G#	A	B	B-D#-F#-A	B7
F	C	D	E	F	G	A	Bb	C	C-E-G-Bb	C7
F#	C#	D#	E#	F#	G#	A#	B	C#	C#-E#-G#-B	C#7
Gb	Db	Eb	F	Gb	Ab	Bb	Cb	Db	Db-F-Ab-Cb	Db7
G	D	E	F#	G	A	B	C	D	D-F#-A-C	D7
Ab	Eb	F	G	Ab	Bb	C	Db	Eb	Eb-G-Bb-Db	Eb7
A	E	F#	G#	A	B	C#	D	E	E-G#-B-D	E7
Bb	F	G	A	Bb	C	D	Eb	F	F-A-C-Eb	F7
B	F#	G#	A#	B	C#	D#	E	F#	F#-A#-C#-E	F#7

F# and Gb major scales are enharmonic, as are the C# and Db Dominant scales.

Recap - Chords, Triads and Intervals

Here is a recap of what we have learned about chords, triads and intervals.

Major chords, such as C, E, F, G, etc., consist of a triad made up of a major third followed by a minor third. For example: a C chord is made up of three notes, C-E-G, making a triad. That triad consists of two thirds as it is three notes from C to E, C-D-E, and three notes from E to G, E-F-G. The first third is a major third because the E is two whole steps above the C. The second third is a minor third with the G one and a half steps above the E, because of the natural half-step between the E and the F, E-F-G.

Scale Degree:	1	2	3	4	5	6	7	1-3-5	
C Major Scale:	C	D	E	F	G	A	B	C-E-G	C major chord
Major Scale Intervals:		w	w	h	w	w	w		
C Chord Triad:	C		E		G				
Stacked Thirds:	Major Third							Two whole steps – 4 semitones	
			Minor Third					One and a half steps – 3 semitones	
	Perfect 5th							7 semitones	

Major 7th chords, such as Cmaj7, Gmaj7, etc., consist of a major third, a minor third and another major third.

Scale Degree:	1	2	3	4	5	6	7	1-3-5-7	
C Major Scale:	C	D	E	F	G	A	B	C-E-G-B	CMaj7 chord
Major Scale Intervals:		w	w	h	w	w	w		
CMaj7 Chord Tones:	C		E		G		B		
Stacked Thirds:	Major Third							Two whole steps – 4 semitones	
			Minor Third					One and a half steps – 3 semitones	
					Major Third			Two whole steps – 4 semitones	
	Major 7th							11 semitones	

The **7th, or dominant 7th, chord** is a major chord with a minor 7th, that is, a major third and a minor third followed by another minor third. Examples are C7, G7, etc.

Scale Degree:	1	2	3	4	5	6	b7	1-3-5-b7	
C Major Scale:	C	D	E	F	G	A	Bb	C-E-G-Bb	C7 chord
Major Scale Intervals:		w	w	h	w	w	h		
C7 Chord Tones:	C		E		G		Bb		
Stacked Thirds:	Major Third							Two whole steps – 4 semitones	
		Minor Third						One and a half steps – 3 semitones	
				Minor Third				One and a half steps- 3 semitones	
		Minor 7th						10 semitones	

Minor chords, such as Dm, Em, Am, etc., consist of a triad made up of a minor third followed by a major third. For example: an A minor chord is made up of three notes, A-C-E, making a triad. That triad is made of two thirds as it is three notes from A to C, A-B-C, and three notes from C to E, C-D-E. The first third is a minor third because the C is one and a half steps above the A, because of the natural half-step between the B and the C, A-B-C. The second third is a major third with the E two whole steps above the C.

Scale Degree:	1	2	b3	4	5	b6	b7	1-b3-5	
A Minor Scale:	A	B	C	D	E	F	G	A-C-E	Am chord
Minor Scale Intervals:		w	h	w	w	h	w		
A Minor Chord Triad:	A		C		E				
Stacked Thirds:	Minor Third							One and a half steps – 3 semitones	
		Major Third						Two whole steps – 4 semitones	
	Perfect 5th							7 semitones	

88

The **minor 7th chord** is a minor chord with an added minor 7th: minor third, major third, minor third. For example, Cm7, Fm7, etc.

Scale Degree:	1	2	♭3	4	5	♭6	♭7	1-♭3-5-♭7	
C Minor Scale:	C	D	E♭	F	G	A♭	B♭	C-E♭-G-B♭	Cm7 chord
Minor Scale Intervals:		w	h	w	w	h	w		
Cm7 Chord Tones:	C		E♭		G		B♭		
Stacked Thirds:	Minor Third							One and a half steps – 3 semitones	
			Major Third					Two whole steps – 4 semitones	
					Minor Third			One and a half steps – 3 semitones	
	Minor 7th							10 semitones	

The **minor Major 7th chord** is a minor chord with an added major 7th: minor third, major third, major third; such as EmMaj7, CmMaj7, etc.

Scale Degree:	1	2	♭3	4	5	♭6	7	1-♭3-5-7	
C Harmonic Minor Scale:	C	D	E♭	F	G	A♭	B	C-E♭-G-B	CmMaj7 chord
Intervals:		w	h	w	w	h	wh		
CmMaj7 Chord Tones:	C		E♭		G		B		
Stacked Thirds:	Minor Third							One and a half steps – 3 semitones	
			Major Third					Two whole steps – 4 semitones	
					Major Third			Two whole steps – 4 semitones	
	Major 7th							11 semitones	

We can see from this how important the intervals of the scale are. The intervals and the natural step-pattern of the scale underlie chords, giving us the major and minor thirds that are stacked to form chords. You can see how interconnected things are in music theory; chords and intervals and scales and scale degrees are all interwoven and interdependent.

Chord Shapes

Chord tones occur in various positions all over the bass fretboard. Here are the note positions of the C7 chord:

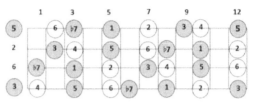

From these patterns we can derive some basic chord shapes. Chord shapes are recurring and the same chord shape can be played for any chord in any key; a G major chord has the same shape as a C major chord.

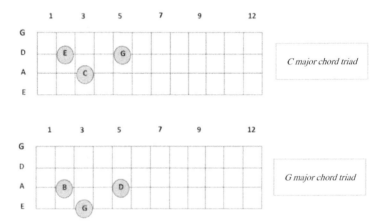

C major chord triad

G major chord triad

Major Chord Shapes:

For simplicity, the chord shapes shown are for the C major chord (with chord tones for the C7 chord) only. All major chords share these patterns.

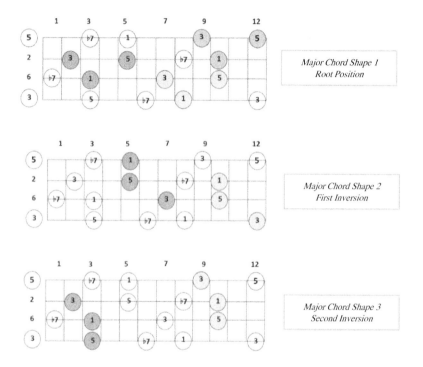

Major Chord Shape 1
Root Position

Major Chord Shape 2
First Inversion

Major Chord Shape 3
Second Inversion

Minor Chord Shapes:

For simplicity, the chord shapes shown are for the Am chord (with chord tones for Am7) only. All minor chords share these patterns.

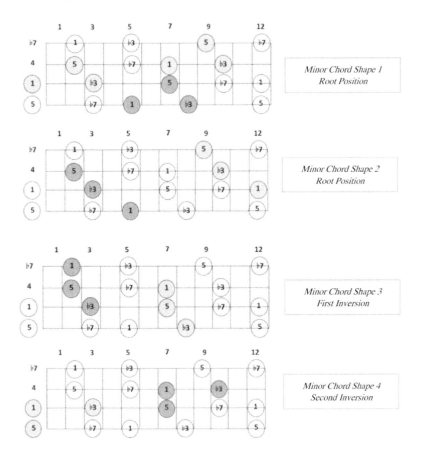

Minor Chord Shape 1
Root Position

Minor Chord Shape 2
Root Position

Minor Chord Shape 3
First Inversion

Minor Chord Shape 4
Second Inversion

There are, of course, many more chord shapes than shown here, but these are the basics and will help you find more patterns on your own.

Chord Inversions

The tones of the chord, the 1-3-5 notes of the scale, can be played with a tone other than the Root in the lowest position. This is called a **Chord Inversion**. Often a songwriter or arranger will want a chord played in an inversion. The chord will be written as C/G to show that the C major chord is to be played with the G note, or fifth, in the lowest position, the second inversion. These are called **Slash Chords**.

- The Root position has the root note in the lowest position.
- The First Inversion has the 3rd of the chord in the lowest position.
- The Second Inversion has the 5th of the chord in the lowest position.
- The Third Inversion has an added chord tone, such as the ♭7, in the lowest position.

		Major Chord Inversions	
Root Position	C	C-E-G	1-3-5
First Inversion		E-G-C	3-5-1
Second Inversion		G-C-E	5-1-3
		Dominant 7th chords	
Root Position	C7	C-E-G-B♭	1-3-5-♭7
First Inversion		E-G-B♭-C	3-5-♭7-1
Second Inversion		G-B♭-C-E	5-♭7-1-3
Third Inversion		B♭-C-E-G	♭7-1-3-5
		Minor Chord Inversions	
Root Position	Am	A-C-E	1-♭3-5
First Inversion		C-E-A	♭3-5-1
Second Inversion		E-A-C	5-1-♭3
		Minor 7th chords	
Root Position	Am7	A-C-E-G	1-♭3-5-♭7
First Inversion		C-E-G-A	♭3-5-♭7-1
Second Inversion		E-G-A-C	5-♭7-1-♭3
Third Inversion		G-A-C-E	♭7-1-♭3-5

The inversions follow a regular pattern. The notes are kept in order, just the starting with a different note and the other notes moved to the end of the line. Root position – 1-3-5-♭7 – this is the natural order of the chord tones.

- First inversion – 3-5-♭7-1 – in the 1st inversion, the Root is moved to the last position; the 3-5-♭7 maintain their original order.
- Second inversion – 5-♭7-1-3 – in the 2nd inversion, the 3 is moved to the last position after the root.
- Third Inversion – ♭7-1-3-5 – in the 3rd inversion, the 5 is moved to the last position; the 1-3-5 maintain their original order.

Notice that the notes are rotated into the lowest position, keeping the root position order. We don't get inversions such as 5-1-♭7-3 or ♭7-5-3-1.

Second Inversions are nearly always followed by the chord with the root of the lowest note in the inversion; for example, C/G, a C major chord with G in the lowest position, is usually followed by a G major chord.

Chord Note Chart – Major and Minor

Here is a chart of the notes of the Major, 7th, Major 7th, Minor and Minor 7th chords in thirteen keys:

Chord:	Major	7th	Major 7		Minor	Minor 7th
Chord Tones:	1-3-5	1-3-5-b7	1-3-5-7		1-b3-5	1-b3-5-b7
C	C-E-G	C-E-G-Bb	C-E-G-B	Cm	C-Eb-G	C-Eb-G-Bb
Db	Db-F-Ab	Db-F-Ab-B	Db-F-Ab-C	Dbm	Db-E-Ab	Db-E-Ab-B
D	D-F#-A	D-F#-A-C	D-F#-A-C#	Dm	D-F-A	D-F-A-C
Eb	Eb-G-Bb	Eb-G-Bb-Db	Eb-G-Bb-D	Ebm	Eb-Gb-Bb	Eb-Gb-Bb-Db
E	E-G#-B	E-G#-B-D	E-G#-B-D#	Em	E-G-B	E-G-B-D
F	F-A-C	F-A-C-Eb	F-A-C-E	Fm	F-Ab-C	F-Ab-C-Eb
F#	F#-A#-C#	F#-A#-C#-E	F#-A#-C#-F	F#m	F#-A-C#	F#-A-C#-E
Gb	Gb-Bb-Db	Gb-Bb-Db-E	Gb-Bb-Db-F	Gbm	Gb-A-Db	Gb-A-Db-E
G	G-B-D	G-B-D-F	G-B-D-F#	Gm	G-Bb-D	G-Bb-D-F
Ab	Ab-C-Eb	Ab-C-E-Gb	Ab-C-Eb-G	Abm	Ab-B-Eb	Ab-B-Eb-Gb
A	A-C#-E	A-C#-E-G	A-C#-E-G#	Am	A-C-E	A-C-E-G
Bb	Bb-D-F	Bb-D-F-Ab	Bb-D-F-A	Bbm	Bb-Db-F	Bb-Db-F-Ab
B	B-D#-F#	B-D#-F#-A	B-D#-F#-A#	Bm	B-D-F#	B-D-F#-A

F# and Gb are enharmonic

Other Chords and Extensions

Besides Majors, Minors and 7th chords you will come across many other chord forms and chord extensions used in songwriting: augmented, diminished, suspended, and so on. All of these chord forms are simply variations of the basic triad, created by making one of the notes of the triad sharp or flat, or by adding or omitting other harmonious tones. The more notes that are added to a chord, the less defined it becomes.

Slash Chords

We encountered **Slash Chords** in the section on *Chord Inversions.* Slash Chords denote chord inversions where a note other than the Root is played in the lowest position. C/G indicates a C major chord played with the fifth note, G, played in the lowest position.

Inversions don't change any notes of the chord, simply the order in which they are played. The normal position of the notes in a C chord is C-E-G, with the root C as the lowest note. When the chord is played in the second inversion, it is played G-C-E, with the fifth G note as the lowest, noted as C/G.

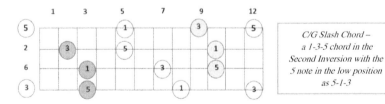

C/G Slash Chord –
a 1-3-5 chord in the
Second Inversion with the
5 note in the low position
as 5-1-3

Slash Chords are also used for Secondary Dominants (there is a chapter on *Secondary Dominants* in the section on *Songs*). Secondary Dominants are borrowed chords substituting the 5th, or Dominant, for a scale chord. They are written as V/ii, V/iii, V/IV, V/V, V/Vi.

Power Chords

In some rock music you may encounter 5th Chords, also called Dyads or **Power Chords**. A Fifth Chord is simply the 1 and 5 of the scale – a chord played without the third. In C, the Power Chord is C-G (often played with the octave as C-G-C). You may sometimes hear them referred to as bare fifth, open fifth or empty fifth chords.

Scale Degrees:	1	2	3	4	5	6	7	8
C Major Scale:	C	D	E	F	G	A	B	C
	Perfect Fifth							

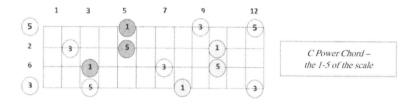

C Power Chord – the 1-5 of the scale

Augmented Chords

A major chord consists of a major third followed by a minor third. We can also have a major third followed by a major third, which gives us an **Augmented Chord** with a sharp 5. They are written as Caug, Caug5 or C+:

Scale Degrees:	1	2	3	4	5#	6	7	8
C Augmented:	C	D	E	F	G#	A	B	C
Caug5 Intervals:	Major Third							
		Major Third						
	Augmented 5th							

Other notes besides the 5th can be augmented, but unless otherwise noted, an augmented chord means an augmented 5th. In an Augmented Chord, the fifth note (5) of the major chord is raised a half tone to make it sharp (5♯). An Augmented triad is: 1-3-5♯.

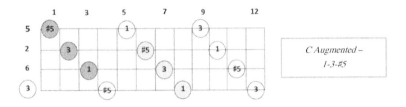

After the 5th, the 4th is the most commonly augmented tone. An augmented 4th chord would be written Caug4.

Scale Degrees:	1	2	3	4♯	5	6	7	8
C Augmented 4:	C	D	E	F♯	G	A	B	C
Caug4 Intervals:	Major 3rd							
		Major 2nd						
	Augmented 4th							

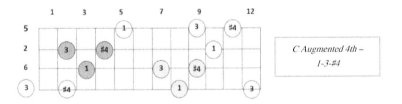

Suspended Chords

Suspended Chords have the 3rd replaced, usually by the 4th, but sometimes the 2nd. They are written as Csus or Csus4 when the 4th is used and Csus2 when the 2nd is used.

A Suspended Chord is 1-4-5 or 1-2-5. The sus4 is the only chord that uses the 4th note of the scale (other than 11 chords) and the sus2 is the only one that uses the 2nd note of the scale (other than 9, 11 and 13 chords).

Scale Degrees:	**1**	2	3	**4**	**5**	6	7	8
C Major Scale:	**C**	D	E	**F**	**G**	A	B	C
Sus4 Intervals:	Perfect 4th							
	Perfect 5th							

Scale Degrees:	**1**	**2**	3	4	**5**	6	7	8
C Major Scale:	**C**	**D**	E	F	**G**	A	B	C
Sus2 Intervals:	Major 2nd							
		Perfect 4th						
	Perfect 5th							

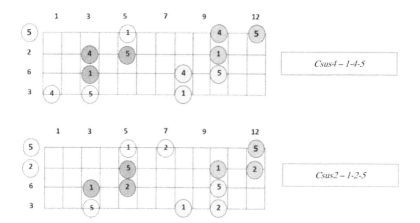

Csus4 – 1-4-5

Csus2 – 1-2-5

Chord Note Chart – Power, Aug, Sus

	Power chord		Augmented			Augmented 4			Sus2			Sus4		
	1	5	1	3	♯5	1	3	♯4	1	2	5	1	4	5
C	C	G	C	E	G♯	C	E	F♯	C	D	G	C	F	G
D♭	D♭	A♭	D♭	F	A	D♭	F	G	D♭	E♭	A♭	D♭	G♭	A♭
D	D	A	D	F♯	A♯	D	F♯	G♯	D	E	A	D	G	A
E♭	E♭	B♭	E♭	G	B	E♭	G	A	E♭	F	B♭	E♭	A♭	B♭
E	E	B	E	G♯	C	E	G♯	A♯	E	F♯	B	E	A	B
F	F	C	F	A	C♯	F	A	B	F	G	C	F	B♭	C
F♯	F♯	C♯	F♯	A♯	D	F♯	A♯	C	F♯	G♯	C♯	F♯	B	C♯
G♭	G♭	D♭	G♭	B♭	D	G♭	B♭	C	G♭	A♭	D♭	G♭	C♭	D♭
G	G	D	G	B	D♯	G	B	C♯	G	A	D	G	C	D
A♭	A♭	E♭	A♭	C	E	A♭	C	D	A♭	B♭	E♭	A♭	D♭	E♭
A	A	E	A	C♯	E♯	A	C♯	D♯	A	B	E	A	D	E
B♭	B♭	F	B♭	D	G♭	B♭	D	E	B♭	C	F	B♭	E♭	F
B	B	F♯	B	D♯	G	B	D♯	E♯	B	C♯	F♯	B	E	F♯

F♯ and G♭ are enharmonic

100

Diminished and Half-Diminished Chords

A minor chord is a minor third followed by a major third. When a minor third is followed by another minor third, it is called a **Diminished Chord** with a flat 5. It is often written as Cdim, C° or Cm♭5:

Scale Degrees:	1	2	♭3	4	♭5	♭6	♭♭7	8	1-♭3-♭5	
C Diminished:	C	D	E♭	F	G♭	A♭	B♭♭	C	C-E♭-G♭	C° chord
	Minor Third									
Cdim Intervals:		Minor Third								
	Diminished 5th									

Other notes can be diminished, but unless noted otherwise, a diminished chord refers to a diminished 5th. (To see why it is called a diminished 5th, see the chapter on *Augmented and Diminished Intervals*).

A Diminished Chord with a flat 7 is called a Half-Diminished Chord.

A minor 7th chord consists of a minor third followed by a major third; stacking another minor third on top gives us a flat 7, an interval of a minor 7th.

Scale Degree:	1	2	♭3	4	5	♭6	♭7	1-♭3-5-♭7	
C minor Scale:	C	D	E♭	F	G	A♭	B♭	C-E♭-G-B♭	Cm7 chord
3 Semitones	Minor Third								
4 Semitones		Major Third							
3 Semitones			Minor Third						
10 Semitones		Minor 7th							

A Diminished Chord uses a flatted third, like a minor chord, and a flatted fifth: 1-♭3-♭5. With a diminished chord, flat fifth, gives us a minor third stacked on a minor third, so when we stack another minor third on top, we end up with a double flat 7, ♭♭7, which is a Diminished 7, making the chord 1-♭3-♭5-♭♭7.

Scale Degree:	1	2	♭3	4	♭5	♭6	♭♭7	1-♭3-♭5-♭♭7	
C Diminished:	C	D	E♭	F	G♭	A♭	B♭♭	C-E♭-G♭-B♭♭	C°7 chord
3 Semitones	Minor Third								
3 Semitones		Minor Third							
3 Semitones			Minor Third						
9 Semitones		Diminished 7th							

To make a chord with a ♭7 we have to stack a major third onto the Diminished 5th to make a Minor 7th. Because a full Diminished 7 has a double flat 7, a chord with one flat 7 is half-diminished.

The ♭♭7 is enharmonic to the 6th of the scale, so why is it called a ♭♭7 instead of just a 6? The reason is because we are dealing with a diminished interval. Calling the note ♭♭7 lets us know that we are using a double-lowered 7th, it communicates its relationship to the other notes in the chord. It may be the same pitch as the 6th, but it is named differently. It's the same as we saw in the G♭ scale: G♭-A♭-B♭-C♭-D♭-E♭-F-G♭. The C♭ is enharmonic to a B natural, but we call it C♭ because in the scale we are using a lowered C.

Scale Degree:	1	♭2	2	♭3	3	4	♭5	5	♭6	6	♭7	7	1-♭3-♭5-♭7
C Scale:	C	D♭	D	E♭	E	F	G♭	G	A♭	B♭♭	B♭	B	C-E♭-G♭-B♭
Semitones:	0	1	2	3	4	5	6	7	8	9	10	11	Cm7♭5
3 Semitones		Minor 3rd											
3 Semitones				Minor 3rd									
6 Semitones		Diminished 5th											
3 Semitones							Minor 3rd						
9 Semitones		Diminished 7th											
4 Semitones							Major 3rd						
10 Semitones		Minor 7th											

A diminished 7 chord is written:

Cdim7 or with °, as in C°7 = 1-♭3-♭5-♭♭7 (6) = C-E♭-G♭-B♭♭.

A half-diminished 7 chord is written:

Cm7♭5 or with ø, as in Cø = 1-♭3-♭5-♭7 = C-E♭-G♭-B♭.

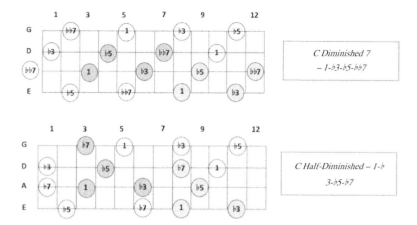

Chord Note Chart – Dim, Dim7, Half-dim

	Diminished			Diminished 7				Half-Diminished			
	1	b3	b5	1	b3	b5	bb7	1	b3	b5	b7
C	C	Eb	Gb	C	Eb	Gb	A	C	Eb	Gb	Bb
Db	Db	E	G	Db	E	G	Bb	Db	E	G	B
D	D	F	Ab	D	F	Ab	B	D	F	Ab	C
Eb	Eb	Gb	A	Eb	Gb	A	C	Eb	Gb	A	Db
E	E	G	Bb	E	G	Bb	Db	E	G	Bb	D
F	F	Ab	B	F	Ab	B	D	F	Ab	B	Eb
F#	F#	A	C	F#	A	C	D#	F#	A	C	E
Gb	Gb	A	C	Gb	A	C	Eb	Gb	A	C	E
G	G	Bb	Db	G	Bb	Db	E	G	Bb	Db	F
Ab	Ab	B	D	Ab	B	D	F	Ab	B	D	Gb
A	A	C	Eb	A	C	Eb	Gb	A	C	Eb	G
Bb	Bb	Db	E	Bb	Db	E	G	Bb	Db	E	Ab
B	B	D	F	B	D	F	G#	B	D	F	A

F# and Gb are enharmonic

6ᵗʰ Chords

The 6ᵗʰ chord adds a major 6ᵗʰ to the basic chord triad: 1-3-5-6. In C that's: C-E-G-A. It is written as C6 or Cadd6.

Scale Degrees:	1	2	3	4	5	6	7	8
C Major Scale:	C	D	E	F	G	A	B	C

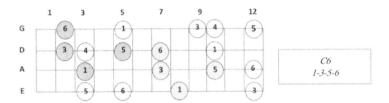

Sixth chords have the same notes as the relative minor seventh chords in the first inversion.

Degree:	1	3	5	6		b3	5	b7	1
C6	C	E	G	A	Am7	C	E	G	A
Db6	Db	F	Ab	Bb	Bbm7	Db	F	Ab	Bb
D6	D	F#	A	B	Bm7	D	F#	A	B
Eb6	Eb	G	Bb	C	Cm7	Eb	G	Bb	C
E6	E	G#	B	C#	C#m7	E	G#	B	C#
F6	F	A	C	D	Dm7	F	A	C	D
F#6	F#	A#	C#	D#	D#m7	F#	A#	C#	D#
Gb6	Gb	Bb	Db	Eb	Ebm7	Gb	Bb	Db	Eb
G6	G	B	D	E	Em7	G	B	D	E
Ab6	Ab	C	Eb	F	Fm7	Ab	C	Eb	F
A6	A	C#	E	F#	F#m7	A	C#	E	F#
Bb6	Bb	D	F	G	Gm7	Bb	D	F	G
B6	B	D#	F#	G#	G#m7	B	D#	F#	G#

F# and Gb are enharmonic

9th, 11th and 13th Chords

The 9th, 11th and 13th Chords are called Added Tone Chords or Upper Extension Chords.

The 9th, 11th and 13th chords are built on the dominant scale and add compound intervals to the basic chord. Compound Intervals are intervals that go beyond the octave. The 9th, 11th and 13th notes are called Tensions, as in extensions. They are non-harmonic non-chord tones that are used in chords to introduce dissonant intervals that cry for resolution.

C	D	E	F	G	A	B	C	D	E	F	G	A
1	2	3	4	5	6	7	8	9	10	11	12	13

The 9th note corresponds to the 2nd, the 11th to the 4th, and the 13th to the 6th. The compound intervals are used because chords are built from stacked thirds.

Scale Degree:	1	2	3	4	5	6	b7	8	9	10	11	12	13	b14	15
C Dominant Scale:	C	D	E	F	G	A	Bb	C	D	E	F	G	A	Bb	C

Major 3rd

Minor 3rd

Minor 3rd

Major 3rd

Minor 3rd

Major 3rd

9th

11th

13th

The 9th, 11th and 13th chords include the ♭7 of the dominant scale. Without the ♭7 they are written as add9, add11 and add13 and use compound intervals of the diatonic scale.

Scale	1	2	3	4	5	6	♭7	8	9	10	11	12	13		
Scale Degree:	1	2	3	4	5	6	♭7	8	9	10	11	12	13	1-3-5-♭7-9	
C Dom Scale:	C	D	E	F	G	A	B♭	C	D	E	F	G	A	C-E-G-B♭-D	C9
Scale Degree:	1	2	3	4	5	6	♭7	8	9	10	11	12	13	1-3-5-9	
C Major Scale:	C	D	E	F	G	A	B♭	C	D	E	F	G	A	C-E-G-D	Cadd9
Scale Degree:	1	2	3	4	5	6	♭7	8	9	10	11	12	13	1-5-♭7-9-11	
C Dom Scale:	C	D	E	F	G	A	B♭	C	D	E	F	G	A	C-G-B♭-D-F	C11
Scale Degree:	1	2	3	4	5	6	♭7	8	9	10	11	12	13	1-5-9-11	
C Major Scale:	C	D	E	F	G	A	B♭	C	D	E	F	G	A	C-G-D-F	Cadd11
Scale Degree:	1	2	3	4	5	6	♭7	8	9	10	11	12	13	1-3-♭7-13	
C Dom Scale:	C	D	E	F	G	A	B♭	C	D	E	F	G	A	C-E-B♭-D-A	C13
Scale Degree:	1	2	3	4	5	6	♭7	8	9	10	11	12	13	1-3-9-13	
C Major Scale:	C	D	E	F	G	A	B♭	C	D	E	F	G	A	C-E-D-A	Cadd13

With 9, add9, 11, add11, 13 and add13 chords, the Root is sometimes not played. With the 11 and add11 chords, the 11th creates a dissonance with the 3rd, so the 3rd is often left out, as it is in a sus4 chord (as the 11th is equivalent to the 4th). The dissonant notes, generally intervals of a second, are called Avoid Notes. A perfect 11th will work with a ♭3, or minor 3rd.

There are many variations of these chords, some with or without the root, some with or without the third and some with or without the fifth. Notes are often left out to make the chords playable as the more notes in a chord the more difficult the fingering becomes. A five note chord is the largest that can be played on a keyboard with one hand, and it is difficult to play more than four notes on a guitar, so chords such as the seven note C13 (1-3-5-♭7-9-11-13) are reduced to the essential defining tones to make them playable. As the defining tones may change depending on the harmony with neighboring chords, the added tone chords can be played in many variations.

The add chords with a 3rd can be made minor by making the 3rd flat. They are written as Cm6, Cm9, etc. It's understood that Cm9 and other added tone chords include the ♭7 so it is not normally written Cm7add 9, although it can be. With a Cm11 or Cm(add 11), it is more likely that the 5 will be left out than the ♭3 as the ♭3 is more of a defining tone for the minor chord than the 5.

Added tone chords can have a major 7 instead of a minor 7 and are written Cmaj7(add9), etc. The 9th, 11th, and 13th extensions can be made sharp or flat, as in ♯9, ♭13, etc.

In C, the 9th note is D, corresponding to the 2nd note of the scale; the 11th, F, is the same as the 4; and the 13th, A, is the same as the 6 – they are simply one octave higher on the musical staff. Those who strictly follow the written music will always play the 9, 11 and 13 notes in their proper positions, but bass players will play the 9, 11 and 13 notes in the 2nd, 4th or 6th positions, depending on what sounds best for that particular bassline.

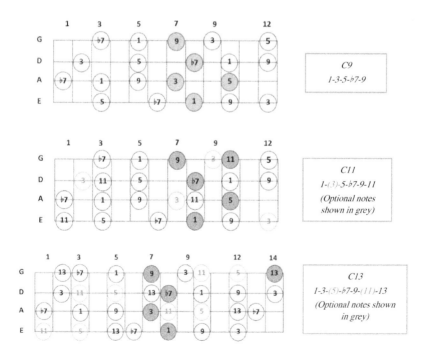

Alt Chords

Alt chords, or altered chords, are used primarily in jazz. They are dominant 7th chords usually with a raised or lowered 5th ($b5$/$\#5$) and altered tensions, such as $b9$, $\#9$, $b11$, $\#11$, $b13$ or $\#13$. Alt $b13$ chords often omit the perfect 5th note to avoid dissonance.

Alt chords add non-scale tones and generally break away from the tertiary harmony of the stacked thirds pattern.

Chord Form Chart

Here is a chart of the notes in the common chord forms:

Scale Degree:	1	2	3	4	5	6	7	9	11	13	
Major	1		3		5						1-3-5
7th (Dominant 7th)	1		3		5		b7				1-3-5-b7
Major 7th	1		3		5		7				1-3-5-7
Minor	1		b3		5						1-b3-5
Minor 7th	1		b3		5		b7				1-b3-5-b7
Augmented	1		3		5#						1-3-5#
Augmented 4	1		3	#4							1-3-#4
Diminished	1		b3		b5						1-b3-b5
Diminished 7th	1		b3		b5	(6)	bb7				1-b3-b5-bb7
Half-diminished	1		b3		b5		b7				1-b3-b5-b7
Suspended	1			4	5						1-4-5
Suspended 2nd	1	2			5						1-2-5
Power Chord	1				5						1-5
6	1		3		5	6					1-3-5-6
9	1	(9)	3		5		b7	9			1-3-5-b7-9
add9	1	(9)	3		5			9			1-3-5-9
11	1	(9)		(11)	5		b7	9	11		1-5-b7-9-11
add11	1	(9)		(11)	5			9	11		1-5-9-11
13	1	(9)	3			(13)	b7	9		13	1-3-b7-9-13
add13	1	(9)	3			(13)		9		13	1-3-9-13

As you can see from this chart, the most common chord forms stay close to the stacked thirds patterns of 1-3-5-b7.

Chord Names

Chord names are always written in the same pattern – the chord root followed by the accidentals, then the quality followed by the extensions and alterations.

- Chord Root = C, E, G, etc.
- Accidentals: ♭ or ♯ = F♯, E♭, etc.
- Quality = minor, suspended, diminished, augmented, etc.
- Extensions = 7th, maj7, etc.
- Alterations = ♭5, ♯4, etc.
- Tensions = add9, add13, etc.

For example, B♭m7♭5 is a B♭ minor triad with a ♭7 and a ♭5.

Unfortunately there is no standard notation for chords. Many variations have arisen over the years resulting in much confusion. Here are the most common forms of notation, all shown in C for simplicity:

Major	C	CMaj	Cmaj	CΔ	
Minor	Cm	Cmi	Cmin	C-	-C
Seventh	C7				
Minor Seventh	Cm7	Cmi7	Cmin7	C-7	-C7
Major Seventh	Cmaj7	CM7	CΔ7	CΔ	C7̶
Augmented	Caug	C+			
Diminished	Cdim	C°	Cm♭5		
Diminished 7th	Cdim7	C°7			
Half-Diminished 7th	Cᵒ̸	Cm7♭5			
Suspended	Csus	Csus4			
6th	C6	Cadd6			
9th	C9	Cadd9			
11th	C11	Cadd9			
13th	C13	Cadd13			

Note: the □ symbol means major. In some notations styles, C□ means a C major chord, but in others, C□ always means a Cmaj7 chord.

Clarifying Terms

Before moving on to the next sections on *Modes*, we will have a little clarification and review. We have three ways of referring to note positions: letters, numbers and intervals.

- The letters are the common note names: A-B-C-D-E-F-G.
- The numbers are the scale degrees: 1-2-3-4-5-6-7.
- The intervals are note distances: 2nd, 3rd, 4th, 5th, 6th, 7th, Octave.

C Major scale:	C	D	E	F	G	A	B	C
Scale Degree:	1	2	3	4	5	6	7	8
Interval: 2nd	2nd							
Interval: 3rd	3rd							
Interval: 4th	4th							
Interval: 5th	5th							
Interval: 6th	6th							
Interval: 7th	7th							
Interval: Octave	O							

Just so there is no confusion over musical terms:

- a **note** (C-D-E, etc.) can be natural (♮), sharp (♯) or flat (♭) – it can't be major or minor. When a note is referred to as major or minor, it is actually the interval that is major or minor, not the note. For example, in a CMaj7 chord, the seventh note of the C scale is B, so B is the major 7th. The root B note is natural (♮), the interval is a major 7th. The note is not called major; it's the interval that is called major.

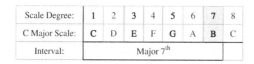

Scale Degree:	1	2	3	4	5	6	7	8
C Major Scale:	C	D	E	F	G	A	B	C
Interval:				Major 7th				

For a C7 chord, the seventh note of the scale, B, is made flat, B♭, which is an interval of a minor 7th. The note is called flat, not minor; the interval is called minor.

Scale Degree:	1	2	3	4	5	6	♭7	8
C Major Scale:	C	D	E	F	G	A	B♭	C
Interval:		Minor 7th						

- a **scale degree** (1-2-3-4-5-6-7) can be natural (♮), sharp (♯) or flat (♭) – it can't be major or minor.
- an **interval** (third, fifth, seventh, etc.) can be major or minor, diminished or augmented, it can't be natural (♮), sharp (♯) or flat (♭).
- a **chord** can be major or minor, and sharp (♯) or flat (♭), and augmented, diminished, suspended, etc.

When we talk about an E♭m7 chord, we say that it is an E♭ minor chord with a flat 7. In E♭, the flat 7 note is D♭, the scale degree would be ♭7, the interval would be a minor 7th.

There are different ways of describing things in musical theory. For example, I have described a major chord as built of stacked thirds, a major third and a minor third. It can also be described as constructed from an interval of a major third and an interval of a perfect fifth; for example, we could say that a C chord, C-E-G, is two stacked thirds, C to E and E to G, but we could also say that it consists of a major third, C to E, and a perfect fifth, C to G. Both approaches result in the same notes for the C chord, C-E-G.

Scale Degree:	1	2	3	4	5	6	7	8
C Major scale:	C	D	E	F	G	A	B	C
Intervals:	Major Third							
	Perfect Fifth							

Modes

Keys and modes are two different approaches to musical structure. The modes we have today come from the Medieval church modes used in plainsong. Modes were the main form of musical composition throughout Medieval and Renaissance times. In the Baroque era, starting in the 16th century, key notation, with the same scale patterns in all keys, was developed resulting in the staff with sharps and flats we use today.

One of the difficulties with modes was that they could not be easily transposed to other keys. This was due to the just intonation and quarter comma meantone temperament tuning systems used at the time which resulted in dissonant intervals. With the development of well-tempered and equal temperament tuning systems in the 16th century, transposition without dissonance became possible.

The introduction of transposable keys coincided with the transition from Renaissance counterpoint, or individual harmonically interdependent voices, to chordal accompaniments. Modal counterpoint of interwoven voices was limited and composition based on melody supported by chords greatly expanded musical range.

With chordal music, only two of the modes were used, the Ionian, which became the major scale, and the Aeolian, which became the minor scale. The rest of the modes were largely forgotten until interest was revived in the 19th century by folksong collectors who discovered that many old English, Irish and Scottish folk songs were in the Dorian mode. In the early 20th century the traditional songs of the Appalachians in the US were collected and they also favored the Dorian mode; because of this, Dorian is known as Mountain Mode in some folk circles. Modes came into prominence in the mid-20th century, first with Bebop and then with modal jazz, popularized by Miles Davis, John Coltrane and others.

Modes were used mainly in jazz improvisation, but renewed interest in modes has led to a number of modal pop songs and it is becoming more important to know the modes to keep up with the development of modern music. Having a basic understanding of modes will help in the overall understanding of music.

Keys and Modes

The difference between keys and modes is quite simple. We know that in key-based music, the notes are adjusted with sharps and flats to make the scale conform to the natural major scale step-pattern so the same scale pattern can be played in any key.

Major Scale Degree:	1	2	3	4	5	6	7	8
Major Scale Step-pattern:		w	w	h	w	w	w	h
D Major Scale:	D	E	F♯	G	A	B	C♯	D

In the key of D major, the natural half-steps between E/F and between B/C are made into whole steps by using sharps so that the D major scale follows the same ···w-w-h-w-w-w-h··· step-pattern as the C major scale. But in modes, the natural half-steps between E/F and B/C are retained and the step-pattern is changed to fit the notes.

Major Scale Degree:	1	2	3	4	5	6	7	8/1	2	3	4	5	6	7	8
Major Scale Step-pattern:	h	w	w	h	w	w	w	h	w	w	h	w	w	w	h
C Major Scale:	C	D	E	F	G	A	B	C	D	E	F	G	A	B	C
Dorian Mode:	C	D	E	F	G	A	B	C	D	E	F	G	A	B	C
Dorian Mode Step-pattern:	h	w	w	h	w	w	w	h	w	w	h	w	w	w	h
Dorian Mode: Degree		1	2	3	4	5	6	7	8						

The half-steps in the 3-4 and 7-8 positions of the major scale are shifted into the 2-3 and 6-7 positions in the Dorian Mode.

Scale Degree:	1	2	3	4	5	6	7	8
Major Scale Step-pattern:		w	w	h	w	w	w	h
Dorian Mode Step-pattern:		w	h	w	w	w	h	w

The diatonic scale step-pattern repeats indefinitely:

···w-w-h-w-w-w-h-w-w-h-w-w-w-h-w-w-h-w-w-w-h···:‖ Repeat

Cut out this chunk and you have a major scale or Ionian mode pattern:

···**w-w-h-w-w-w-h**-w-w-h-w-w-w-h-w-w-h-w-w-w-h···:‖ Repeat

If we start on D and keeping the half-steps between E/F and B/C we get a new step-pattern, or a different chunk cut out of the recurring step-pattern:

···w-**w-h-w-w-w-h-w**-w-h-w-w-w-h-w-w-h-w-w-w-h-w-w-h···:ll Repeat

Each Mode has a unique step-pattern, a new chunk cut out of the recurring step-pattern. When we compare the Dorian mode to the major scale step-pattern, we can say that the Dorian mode has a flat third and a flat seventh.

Major Scale Degree:	1	2	3	4	5	6	7	8
Major Scale Step-pattern:		w	w	h	w	w	w	h
C Major Scale:	C	D	E	F	G	A	B	C
D Dorian Mode:	D	E	F	G	A	B	C	D
Dorian Mode Step-pattern:		w	h	w	w	w	h	w
Dorian Mode Degree:	1	2	♭3	4	5	6	♭7	8

Keys and modes are two different approaches to musical structure. In keys the notes are adjusted to fit the step-pattern so that all scales in all keys use the same patterns; with the modes, the step-pattern changes with each tonic.

Each mode uses exactly the same notes as the root scale; the notes are not adjusted with sharps and flats as they are with scales in different keys.

There are seven modes, corresponding to the seven notes of the diatonic scale: Ionian, Dorian, Phrygian, Lydian, Mixolydian, Aeolian and Locrian. This gives us seven distinct step-patterns. The modes are named after the initial note of the mode, not from the root scale. For example, if the start with C Ionian, the second mode is not C Dorian, but D Dorian as D is the first note of the second mode.

115

Here are the seven modes and their step-patterns, starting with C Ionian:

	1	2	3	4	5	6	7	1	2	3	4	5	6	7
C Ionian (I)	C	D	E	F	G	A	B	C	D	E	F	G	A	B
	h	w	w	h	w	w	w	h	w	w	h	w	w	w

		1	2	b3	4	5	6	b7	8					
D Dorian (II)	C	D	E	F	G	A	B	C	D	E	F	G	A	B
	h	w	w	h	w	w	w	h	w	w	h	w	w	w

			1	b2	b3	4	5	b6	b7	8				
E Phrygian (III)	C	D	E	F	G	A	B	C	D	E	F	G	A	B
	h	w	w	h	w	w	w	h	w	w	h	w	w	w

				1	2	3	#4	5	6	7	8			
F Lydian (IV)	C	D	E	F	G	A	B	C	D	E	F	G	A	B
	h	w	w	h	w	w	w	h	w	w	h	w	w	w

					1	2	3	4	5	6	b7	8		
G Mixolydian (V)	C	D	E	F	G	A	B	C	D	E	F	G	A	B
	h	w	w	h	w	w	w	h	w	w	h	w	w	w

						1	2	b3	4	5	b6	b7	8	
A Aeolian (VI)	C	D	E	F	G	A	B	C	D	E	F	G	A	B
	h	w	w	h	w	w	w	h	w	w	h	w	w	w

							1	b2	b3	4	b5	b6	b7	8
B Locrian (VII)	C	D	E	F	G	A	B	C	D	E	F	G	A	B
	h	w	w	h	w	w	w	h	w	w	h	w	w	w

As you can see, each mode is a different chunk cut out of the recurring step-pattern. Starting on each different scale degree shifts the half-steps into a new position. Every mode has two half-steps; where those half-steps fall determines what mode we are in.

Ionian, Lydian and Mixolydian are the Major Modes. Dorian, Phrygian, Aeolian and Locrian all have a b3 and are the Minor Modes. In popular music, the main modes are Ionian (the major scale), Aeolian (the minor scale) and Mixolydian (dominant 7th chords).

Modes on the Bass Fretboard

We know the Major Scale, or Ionian Mode, pattern in C: C-D-E-F-G-A-B-C

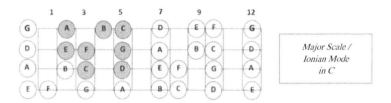

If we apply this step-pattern to D, we get the D major scale: D-E-F#-G-A-B-C#-D

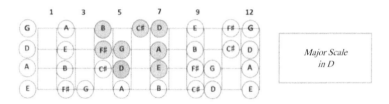

But, if instead of adjusting the half-steps to make D fit the C major scale pattern, we keep the half-steps between E-F and B-C, we get the D Dorian mode: D-E-F-G-A-B-C-D

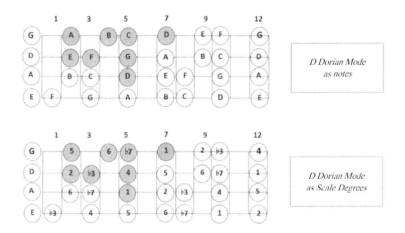

If we do the same for G, keeping the half-steps between B-C and E-F, we get the G Mixolydian mode: G-A-B-C-D-E-F-G

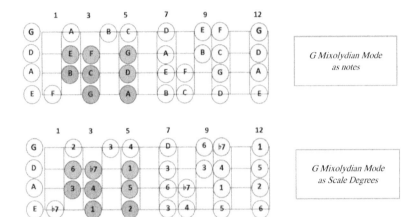

Mode Shapes

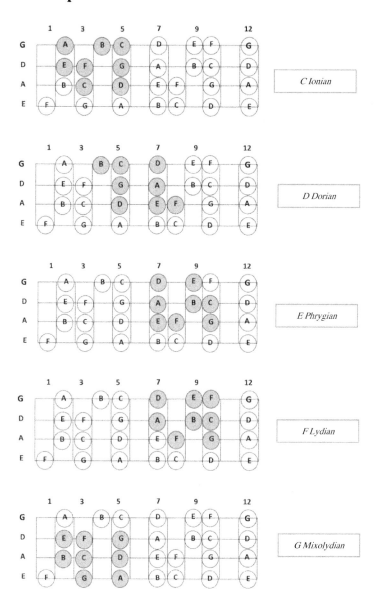

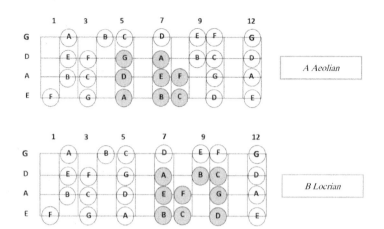

A Aeolian

B Locrian

Modes and Chords

When Key notation was developed, it did not completely replace the Medieval modes, but built on the foundation of Modal composition. Keys and Modes overlap, and this is most evident in chords. We can derive a series of chords from the Modes.

	1	2	3	4	5	6	7	8	1-3-5-7
C Ionian (I) (Major)	C	D	E	F	G	A	B	C	C-E-G-B
	w	w	h	w	w	w	h		Cmaj7

	1	2	b3	4	5	6	b7	8	1-b3-5-b7
D Dorian (II)	D	E	F	G	A	B	C	D	D-F-A-C
	w	h	w	w	w	h	w		Dm7

	1	b2	b3	4	5	b6	b7	8	1-b3-5-b7
E Phrygian (III)	E	F	G	A	B	C	D	E	E-G-B-D
	h	w	w	w	h	w	w		Em7

	1	2	3	#4	5	6	7	8	1-3-5-7
F Lydian (IV)	F	G	A	B	C	D	E	F	F-A-C-E
	w	w	w	h	w	w	h		Fmaj7

	1	2	3	4	5	6	b7	8	1-3-5-b7
G Mixolydian (V) (Dominant)	G	A	B	C	D	E	F	G	G-B-D-F
	w	w	h	w	w	h	w		G7

	1	2	b3	4	5	b6	b7	8	1-b3-5-b7
A Aeolian (VI) (Minor)	A	B	C	D	E	F	G	A	A-C-E-G
	w	h	w	w	h	w	w		Am7

	1	b2	b3	4	b5	b6	b7	8	1-b3-b5-b7
B Locrian (VII)	B	C	D	E	F	G	A	B	B-D-F-A
	h	w	w	h	w	w	w		Bm7b5

This gives us a sequence of chords corresponding to the notes of the major scale. This **Scale of Chords** is essential to understanding songs and song structure.

Scale Degrees:	1	2	3	4	5	6	7
Scale of Notes (in C):	C	D	E	F	G	A	B
Scale of Chords (in C):	Cmaj7	Dm7	Em7	Fmaj7	G7	Am7	Bm7b5

Chords are derived from Modes and if you know your chord tones, then, in a simplistic way, you know your Modes as well. If you play a C chord you are using the 1-3-5 or C-E-G of the C Ionian Mode. If you play a Dominant chord, such as a G7, you are using the Mixolydian Mode. A minor chord, such as Am uses the Aeolian Mode, and possibly the Dorian Mode for an Am7.

Minor Modes and Chords

We can derive a minor Scale of Chords from the modes if we start on the 6th
degree of the major scale and use the Aeolian VI mode as I, Locrian VII as II, etc.

	1	2	b3	4	5	b6	b7	8	1-b3-5-b7
A Aeolian (Im)	A	B	C	D	E	F	G	A	A-C-E-G
		w	h	w	w	h	w	w	Am7

	1	b2	b3	4	b5	b6	b7	8	1-b3-b5-b7
B Locrian (IImb5)	B	C	D	E	F	G	A	B	B-D-F-A
		h	w	w	h	w	w	w	Bm7b5

	1	2	3	4	5	6	7	8	1-3-5-7
C Ionian (III)	C	D	E	F	G	A	B	C	C-E-G-B
		w	w	h	w	w	w	h	Cmaj7

	1	2	b3	4	5	6	b7	8	1-b3-5-b7
D Dorian (IVm)	D	E	F	G	A	B	C	D	D-F-A-C
		w	h	w	w	w	h	w	Dm7

	1	b2	b3	4	5	b6	b7	8	1-b3-5-b7
E Phrygian (Vm)	E	F	G	A	B	C	D	E	E-G-B-D
		h	w	w	w	h	w	w	Em7

	1	2	3	#4	5	6	7	8	1-3-5-7
F Lydian (VI)	F	G	A	B	C	D	E	F	F-A-C-E
		w	w	w	h	w	w	h	Fmaj7

	1	2	3	4	5	6	b7	8	1-3-5-b7
G Mixolydian (VII)	G	A	B	C	D	E	F	G	G-B-D-F
		w	w	h	w	w	h	w	G7

This gives us a scale of chords corresponding to the notes of the minor scale.

Minor Scale Degrees:	1	2	b3	4	5	b6	b7
Scale of Notes (in Am):	A	B	C	D	E	F	G
Scale of Chords (in Am):	Am7	Bm7b5	Cmaj7	Dm7	Em7	Fmaj7	G7

Modes and Keys

For the modes beginning with C Ionian, the half-steps are always between B-C and E-F. But we can have modes based on other scales besides C.

For modes based on other scales, the modes follow the same step-pattern as the C based modes. For example, G Ionian gives us A Dorian, which follows the same step-pattern as D Dorian.

		1	2	b3	4	5	6	b7	8
D Dorian (II) from the C scale		D	E	F	G	A	B	C	D
		w	w	h	w	w	w	h	w

		1	2	b3	4	5	6	b7	8
A Dorian (II) from the G scale		A	B	C	D	E	F#	G	A
		w	w	h	w	w	w	h	w

If we start with E Ionian using the notes of the E scale, we can build the modes in E using the step-patterns from the basic modal forms in C. Notice that with the modes the notes are not adjusted with sharps and flats the way they are for major and minor scales in different keys. Each mode uses the notes of the root scale starting on a new degree, which makes the half-steps naturally fall into the proper positions without adjusting the notes.

	1	2	3	4	5	6	7	1	2	3	4	5	6	7	1-3-5-7
E Ionian (I)	E	F#	G#	A	B	C#	D#	E	F#	G#	A	B	C#	D#	E-G#-B-D#
	h	w	w	h	w	w	w	h	w	w	h	w	w	w	Emaj7
F# Dorian (II)		1	2	b3	4	5	6	b7	8						1-b3-5-b7
		F#	G#	A	B	C#	D#	E	F#						F#-A-C#-E
	h	w	w	h	w	w	w	h	w	w	h	w	w	w	F#m7
G# Phrygian (III)			1	b2	b3	4	5	b6	b7	8					1-b3-5-b7
			G#	A	B	C#	D#	E	F#	G#					G#-B-D#-F#
	h	w	w	h	w	w	w	h	w	w	h	w	w	w	G#m7
A Lydian (IV)				1	2	3	#4	5	6	7	8				1-3-5-7
				A	B	C#	D#	E	F#	G#	A				A-C#-E-G#
	h	w	w	h	w	w	w	h	w	w	h	w	w	w	Amaj7
B Mixolydian (V)					1	2	3	4	5	6	b7	8			1-3-5-b7
					B	C#	D#	E	F#	G#	A	B			B-D#-F#-A
	h	w	w	h	w	w	w	h	w	w	h	w	w	w	B7
C# Aeolian (VI)						1	2	b3	4	5	b6	b7	8		1-b3-5-b7
						C#	D#	E	F#	G#	A	B	C#		C#-E-G#-B
	h	w	w	h	w	w	w	h	w	w	h	w	w	w	C#m7
D# Locrian (VII)							1	b2	b3	4	b5	b6	b7	8	1-b3-5-b7
							D#	E	F#	G#	A	B	C#	D#	D#-F#-A-C#
	h	w	w	h	w	w	w	h	w	w	h	w	w	w	B#m7b5

Parallel Modes

We have looked at modes as a separate mode for each scale degree, C Ionian, D Dorian, E Phrygian, etc. These are called **Relative Modes**. If we begin each mode with the same tonic, we can derive the **Parallel Modes**:

	1	2	3	4	5	6	7	8	1-3-5-7
C Ionian (I) from the C scale	C	D	E	F	G	A	B	C	C-E-G-B
	w	w	h	w	w	w	h		Cmaj7

	1	2	b3	4	5	6	b7	8	1-b3-5-b7
C Dorian (II) from the Bb scale	C	D	Eb	F	G	A	Bb	C	C-Eb-G-Bb
	w	h	w	w	w	h	w		Cm7

	1	b2	b3	4	5	b6	b7	8	1-b3-5-b7
C Phrygian (III) from the Ab scale	C	Db	Eb	F	G	Ab	Bb	C	C-Eb-G-Bb
	h	w	w	w	h	w	w		Cm7

	1	2	3	#4	5	6	7	8	1-3-5-7
C Lydian (IV) from the G scale	C	D	E	F#	G	A	B	C	C-E-G-B
	w	w	w	h	w	w	h		Cmaj7

	1	2	3	4	5	6	b7	8	1-3-5-b7
C Mixolydian (V) from the F scale	C	D	E	F	G	A	Bb	C	C-E-G-Bb
	w	w	h	w	w	h	w		C7

	1	2	b3	4	5	b6	b7	8	1-b3-5-b7
C Aeolian (VI) from the Eb scale	C	D	Eb	F	G	Ab	Bb	C	C-Eb-G-Bb
	w	h	w	w	h	w	w		Cm7

	1	b2	b3	4	b5	b6	b7	8	1-b3-b5-b7
C Locrian (VII) from the Db scale	C	Db	Eb	F	Gb	Ab	Bb	C	C-Eb-Gb-Bb
	h	w	w	h	w	w	w		Cm7b5

Using Modes

It's great knowing the modes, but how do we use them? There is no definite answer to this question, it depends on the situation. Chords are derived from the modes so they are interconnected.

C Ionian (I)	1-3-5-7	C-E-G-B	Cmaj7
D Dorian (IIm)	1-♭3-5-♭7	D-F-A-C	Dm7
E Phrygian (IIIm)	1-♭3-5-♭7	E-G-B-D	Em7
F Lydian (IV)	1-3-5-7	F-A-C-E	Fmaj7
G Mixolydian (V)	1-3-5-♭7	G-B-D-F	G7
A Aeolian (VIm)	1-♭3-5-♭7	A-C-E-G	Am7
B Locrian (VIIdim)	1-♭3-♭5-♭7	B-D-F-A	Bm7♭5

If a song uses a dominant seventh chord, such as a G7, then you will play a Mixolydian mode over it, with the ♭7. The Dominant scale from which 7th chords are derived is the same as the Mixolydian mode. But suppose a song uses the IIm chord, do you play the Dorian mode over it, or the Aeolian mode, the natural minor scale? It depends on which notes are referenced by the harmony and by the melody.

In many cases it won't matter as the chord tones of 1-♭3-5-♭7, D-F-A-C for Dm7, are the same in the Dorian and Aeolian modes. If you play a minor pentatonic over the IIm7 chord, it doesn't hit the 6th either. The difference is if a major 6th or a flat 6th is referenced, even as a passing note, then the Dorian or Aeolian will be used accordingly. Aeolian is often used with minor chords and Dorian with minor seventh chords.

The same applies to the Phrygian mode (IIIm), the ♭2 is not a chord tone or in the minor pentatonic, so if you stick to the chord tones, it won't matter if you play a natural minor scale or Phrygian mode. For the Lydian mode (IV), the ♯4 is not a chord tone or in the minor pentatonic scale.

For diminished chords, the Locrian mode is applicable as the ♭5 is a chord tone, but whether you reference the ♭2 of the Locrian as well or use a major 2nd depends on the context, on what is appropriate for the song you are playing.

This approach is very basic; to really use modes effectively requires a more advanced understanding of harmonic function. Incorporating modes into an accompaniment may require some coordination with the other band members to avoid discordance.

Part II

Songs

When playing a bass accompaniment, you will notice that many songs share the same groups of chords. You will also notice that the chord groups can be very different. If you are playing a song that includes C, F and G, it may go to E minor. But another song with D, G and A may go to the F# minor. Why does the F#m fit in with the second progression, but not with the first? Why are certain chords grouped together?

If you are a bass player, at some point you will be learning a new song and the keyboard player will say, "It's a three chord progression in G. The chorus goes to the fourth and the bridge starts on the minor sixth and then goes back to the one. It's easy." Or you will be jamming with some friends and the guitar player will say, "I've worked out a really cool riff in E♭ minor; listen to this!" Or you have learned a song in the key of D from a recording or tabs and the singer suddenly says she wants it in B♭ to better suit her voice. What do you do?

Understanding song structure and how the chords and different elements of songs relate to one another will help you out in these situations, especially when jamming or improvising or learning new material because you will know what chord groups to expect. Songs range from extremely simple to extremely complex, but even the simplest song can be an opportunity for some exciting bass work.

The Scale of Chords

In the sections *Modes and Major Chords* and *Modes and Minor Chords*, we saw that each scale degree has an accompanying chord derived from the Modes giving us a **Scale of Chords** for both major and minor keys. The Scale of Chords gives us a series of chords that harmonize together within a given key. The Scale of Chords is the secret heart of melodic music.

Scale Degrees:	1	2	3	4	5	6	7
Scale of Notes (in C):	C	D	E	F	G	A	B
Scale of Chords (in C):	C	Dm	Em	F	G	Am	Bm♭5

Songs consist of a melody accompanied by chords, called a **Chord Progression**. The Scale of Chords lists all the common chords in a given key – almost all songs will be composed of some combination of the principle chords of that key. Knowing the Scale of Chords gives insight into the building blocks of a song. The Scale of Chords explains why certain chords are grouped together, why a song using the chords C-F-G might go to an Em, while a song using the chords D-G-A might go to F♯m.

In the Scale of Chords some of the chords are major and some are minor. For the Scale of Chords in a major key, the first chord is major, the 2nd and 3rd chords are minor, the 4th and 5th chords are major, the 6th is minor and the 7th is diminished, a sequence we can write out as M-m-m-M-M-m-m♭5 (with M = Major and m = minor).

Scale of Chords (in C):	C	Dm	Em	F	G	Am	Bm♭5
Major Scale Chord Pattern:	M	m	m	M	M	m	m♭5

This gives us a pattern that is the same for all major keys. For example, the G tonic scale is G-A-B-C-D-E-F♯, so following the same major and minor pattern, the Scale of Chords in G is G-Am-Bm-C-D-Em-F♯°.

Scale of Notes (in G):	G	A	B	C	D	E	F♯
Scale of Chords (in G):	G	Am	Bm	C	D	Em	F♯m♭5
Major Scale Chord Pattern:	M	m	m	M	M	m	m♭5

This pattern of chords is not set in stone and there is an enormous amount of variation in songs where chords can be altered, extended, borrowed or substituted, but these are the principle chords available in the key. If you are in the key of C it is unlikely that you will encounter an F#m chord, because F# is not a scale tone in the key of C, but F# is a scale tone in the keys of D and E so you can expect an F#m in the key of D, where it is the minor third chord, and in the key of E, where it is the minor second chord.

You can see in these three examples how the Scale of Chords relates to the Scale of Notes:

Scale Degrees:	1	2	3	4	5	6	7
Scale of Notes in C:	C	D	E	F	G	A	B
Scale of Chords in C:	C	Dm	Em	F	G	Am	Bmb5
Scale of Notes in D:	D	E	F#	G	A	B	C#
Scale of Chords in D:	D	Em	F#m	G	A	Bm	C#mb5
Scale of Notes in E:	E	F#	G#	A	B	C#	D#
Scale of Chords in E:	E	F#m	G#m	A	B	C#m	D#mb5

The seventh chord is diminished, in C it's Bdim or B° or Bmb5, but in practice the diminished form of the chord is not often used in popular songwriting, it is usually replaced by the flatted seventh chord. In the key of C, the flatted seventh is Bb – there's a section following called *The bVII Chord* that discusses this further.

Besides the bVII, songs will also use the flatted third. The flat third and flat seventh chords are not natural to the major chord scale, although they are natural to the minor chord scale; for this reason, when used in the major scale of chords, it can be said that the flat third and flat seventh are borrowed from the parallel minor scale of chords. This is called **Modal Interchange**.

Scale Degrees:	1	2	3	4	5	6	7
Scale of Notes in C:	C	D	E	F	G	A	B
Scale of Chords in C:	C	Dm	Em	F	G	Am	Bmb5
Scale of Notes in Cm:	C	D	Eb	F	G	Ab	Bb
Scale of Chords in Cm:	Cm	Dmb5	**Eb**	Fm	Gm	Ab	**Bb**

In the key of C the flat third is E♭ and the flat seven is B♭, so the complete scale of chords in C major is:

C	Dm	E♭	Em	F	G	Am	B♭	Bm♭5

Songs in the key of C will almost always be composed of some arrangement of the C-Dm-E♭-Em-F-G-Am-B♭-B° chords and their extensions. So if you are playing a song in the key of C major, these are the chords you can expect to encounter.

Chord Notation

While notes in a scale are given numbers, 1-2-3-4-5-6-7, chords are usually represented by Roman Numerals: I-II-III-IV-V-VI-VII, called Roman Numeral Analysis. Since chords are numbered according to their position in the scale, the scale of chords in numerical notation would be written as:

Scale Degree:	1	2	3	4	5	6	7
C Major Scale of Notes:	C	D	E	F	G	A	B
C Major Scale of Chords:	C	Dm	Em	F	G	Am	Bmb5
Chord Scale Degree:	I	IIm	IIIm	IV	V	VIm	VIImb5

We can add the common optional chords bIII and bVII:

C	Dm	Eb	Em	F	G	Am	Bb	Bmb5
I	IIm	bIII	IIIm	IV	V	VIm	bVII	VIImb5

There are several forms of numerical chord notation:

I	IIm	bIII	IIIm	IV	V	VIm	bVII	VIImb5	- minor chords designated by 'm', flats by 'b'
I	ii	bIII	iii	IV	V	vi	bVII	viidim	- minor chords are shown in lower case
I	2m	b3	3m	4	5	6m	b7	7dim	- numbers instead of Roman Numerals
I	2-	b3	3-	4	5	6-	b7	7dim	- Nashville Notation using numbers; minor chords noted with a minus sign, flats by 'b'
I	2		3	4	5	6			- for simple arrangements where it is understood that the II, III & VI are always minor, and the bIII, bVII and VIImb5 are never used

The most popular form of Roman Numeral Analysis is to use upper case for major chords, I-IV-V, and lower case for minor chords, ii-iii-vi. In this book I have opted to use all upper case and indicate minor chords with 'm', IIm-IIIm-VIm. The reason for this is that when discussing chords in written paragraphs the lower case ii, iii, vi minor chords tend to get lost in the body text, while the upper case IIm, IIIm, VIm minor chords stand out a bit more. That's the only reason: for clarity; not because one system is better than or preferable to another.

Scale of Chords in Thirteen Major Keys:

The Scale of Chords in Thirteen Major Keys is as follows (including the ♭III and ♭VII):

	I	IIm	♭III	IIIm	IV	V	VIm	♭VII	VIImb5
C	C	Dm	E♭	Em	F	G	Am	B♭	Bm♭5
D♭	D♭	E♭m	E	Fm	G♭	A♭	B♭m	B	Cm♭5
D	D	Em	F	F♯m	G	A	Bm	C	C♯m♭5
E♭	E♭	Fm	G♭	Gm	A♭	B♭	Cm	D♭	Dm♭5
E	E	F♯m	G	G♯m	A	B	C♯m	D	D♯m♭5
F	F	Gm	A♭	Am	B♭	C	Dm	E♭	Em♭5
F♯	F♯	G♯m	A	A♯m	B	C♯	D♯m	E	Fm♭5
G♭	G♭	A♭m	A	B♭m	B	D♭	E♭m	E	Fm♭5
G	G	Am	B♭	Bm	C	D	Em	F	F♯m♭5
A♭	A	B♭m	B	Cm	D♭	E♭	Fm	G♭	Gm♭5
A	A	Bm	C	C♯m	D	E	F♯m	G	G♯m♭5
B♭	B♭	Cm	D♭	Dm	E♭	F	Gm	A♭	Am♭5
B	B	C♯m	D	D♯m	E	F♯	G♯m	A	A♯m♭5

F♯ and G♭ are enharmonic.

Scale of Chords Relative Minors

We saw in the section on the *Minor Scale Pattern* that every Major Scale has a Relative Minor starting on the 6th degree of the scale. The Major Scale of Chords has a relative minor Scale of Chords as well.

	I	IIm	IIIm	IV	V	VIm	VII°	I	IIm	IIIm	IV	V	VIm	VII°
Chord Scale in C:	C	Dm	Em	F	G	Am	B°	C	Dm	Em	F	G	Am	B°
Chord Scale in Am:	C	Dm	Em	F	G	Am	B°	C	Dm	Em	F	G	Am	B°

The relative minor of C is Am. The Am scale of chords, the relative minor of C, starts on the VIm of the C scale and uses the same chords as the C major scale of chords. All relative minors start on the VIm of the relative major scale.

The major keys and their relative minors are:

Major Key:	C	D	E	F	G	A	B
Relative Minor:	Am	Bm	C#m	Dm	Em	F#m	G#m

The Minor Scale of Chords

The major and relative minor Scale of Chords have the same numeral notation; for example, in the C scale C is I and Am is VIm. In the Am scale of chords, C is usually written as I and Am as VIm, but Am can also be written as Im, or i.

We know the Scale of Chords for the C major key is:

I	IIm	IIIm	IV	V	VIm	VII° (VIImb5)
I	ii	iii	IV	V	vi	vii° (viib5)
C	Dm	Em	F	G	Am	B° (Bmb5)

The Scale of Chords for the A minor key can be written as:

VIm	VIImb5	I	IIm	IIIm	IV	V
vi	viib5	I	ii	iii	IV	V
Am	Bmb5	C	Dm	Em	F	G

or as:

Im	IImb5	III	IVm	Vm	VI	VII
i	iib5	III	iv	v	VI	VII
Am	Bmb5	C	Dm	Em	F	G

The minor Scale of Chords uses the same major and minor sequence of chords as the major Scale of Chords, just in different positions resulting from starting on the VIm of the major scale – in this case, the Am. As you can see, in the minor scale, the positions of the major and minor chords are reversed, except for the II chord, which has a minor function in both. In the major scale, the I-IV-V chords are major and the IIm, IIIm, VIm and VIImb5 are all minor.But in the minor scale, the Im-IImb5-IVm-Vm are all minor chords while the III, VI and VII are major chords. In the table below, the major chords are shown in bold:

Major Chord Scale:	I	IIm	IIIm	**IV**	**V**	VIm	VII°
Minor Chord Scale:	Im	IImb5	**III**	IVm	Vm	**VI**	**VII**

- The sequence of chords in the major scale of chords is:
  M-m-m-M-M-m-mb5.
- The sequence of chords in the minor scale of chords is:
  m-mb5-M-m-m-M-M
  (with M = Major and m = minor).

In the minor scale, the fifth chord is minor, Gm (in Cm). The Vm doesn't have the same strong return to the tonic as the V dominant in the major scale, so the five chord in the minor scale is often replaced by a V major.

Scale of Chords in Thirteen Minor Keys:

The Scale of Chords for thirteen minor keys (shown with the notation in two forms, with Im as in the minor scale and as VIm as in the relative major scale):

	VIm	VIImb5	I	IIm	IIIm	IV	V
	Im	IImb5	III	IVm	Vm	VI	VII
Am	Am	Bmb5	C	Dm	Em	F	G
Bbm	Bbm	Cmb5	Db	Ebm	Fm	Gb	Ab
Bm	Bm	C#mb5	D	Em	F#m	G	A
Cm	Cm	Dmb5	Eb	Fm	Gm	Ab	Bb
C#m	C#m	D#mb5	E	F#m	G#m	A	B
Dm	Dm	Emb5	F	Gm	Am	Bb	C
D#m	D#m	Fmb5	F#	G#m	A#m	B	C#
Ebm	Ebm	Fmb5	Gb	Abm	Bbm	B	Db
Em	Em	F#mb5	G	Am	Bm	C	D
Fm	Fm	Gmb5	Ab	Bbm	Cm	Db	Eb
F#m	F#m	G#mb5	A	Bm	C#m	D	E
Gm	Gm	Amb5	Bb	Cm	Dm	Eb	F
G#m	G#m	A#mb5	B	C#m	D#m	E	F#

The keys of D#m and Ebm are enharmonic.
D#m and Ebm are the relative minors of the enharmonic major keys F# and Gb.

136

Scale of Chords and Harmony

We can begin to understand the harmony of the scale of chords by looking at some relationships. There are six principle chords in the C major scale of chords:

I	IIm	IIIm	IV	V	VIm
C	Dm	Em	F	G	Am

If we look at the three major chords of the scale of chords in C, we see they are C-F-G. The relative minors of C-F-G are Am-Dm-Em.

Major Key:	C	D	E	F	G	A	B
Relative Minor:	Am	Bm	C#m	Dm	Em	F#m	G#m

If we plug the relative minors into the C progression we get: C-Dm-Em-F-G-Am or I-IIm-IIIm-IV-V-VIm, the progression of the Scale of Chords.

	I	IIm	IIIm	IV	V	VIm	I
Major Chords:	C			F	G		C
Minor Chords:		Dm	Em			Am	

The IIm (Dm) is the relative minor of the IV (F) chord; the IIIm (Em) is the relative minor of the V (G) chord; and the VIm (Am) is the relative minor of the I (C) chord. So the six principal chords in any key are the three major chords, I, IV and V, and their relative minors.

The chords share scale notes, which tie them together harmonically. Each chord tone can be found in three other chords in the scale. C is in C, F, Am; D is in Dm, G, Bmb5; E is in C, Em, Am; F is in F, Dm, Bmb5, etc:

Degree:	I	IIm	IIIm	IV	V	VIm	VIImb5
Chords:	C	Dm	Em	F	G	Am	Bmb5
Fifth	G	A	B	C	D	E	F
Third	E	F	G	A	B	C	D
Root	C	D	E	F	G	A	B

The Circle of Fifths

The table of chords in the chapter *Scale of Chords in Thirteen Major Keys* presented above is a linear presentation of the **Circle of Fifths**, also called the Cycle of Fifths. At least, it is called the Circle of Fifths if you go around in a clockwise direction. If you go around counterclockwise it is called the **Circle of Fourths**. The Circle of Fifths is one of the most useful tools in music and learning how to use it will help you through many situations.

The Circle of Fifths is a way of grouping complimentary chords together. It looks like this:

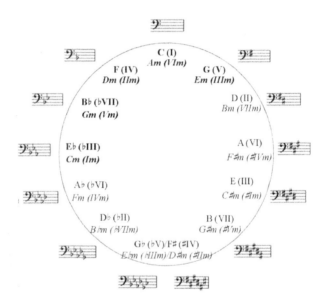

If you count up the keys around the circle, and count the enharmonic keys of G♭ and F♯ as one, you will see that there are twelve keys.

It's called the Circle of Fifths because if you travel in a clockwise direction each chord is the fifth of the previous scale. In the C scale the fifth note is G, and the fifth of the G scale is D, and the fifth of the D scale is A and the fifth of the A scale is E, and so on.

1	2	3	4	5	6	7
C	D	E	F	G	A	B

One Sharp

1	2	3	4	5	6	7
G	A	B	C	D	E	F♯

Two Sharps

1	2	3	4	5	6	7
D	E	F♯	G	A	B	C♯

Three Sharps

1	2	3	4	5	6	7
A	B	C♯	D	E	F♯	G♯

···and so on for the rest of the circle.

Going counter-clockwise, each chord is the fourth of the previous scale: F is the fourth of C, B♭ is the fourth of F, E♭ is the fourth of B♭, and around and around we go.

1	2	3	4	5	6	7
C	D	E	F	G	A	B

One Flat

1	2	3	4	5	6	7
F	G	A	B♭	C	D	E

Two Flats

1	2	3	4	5	6	7
B♭	C	D	E♭	F	G	A

Three Flats

1	2	3	4	5	6	7			
E♭	F	G	A♭	B♭	C	D	E♭	F	G

···and so on for the rest of the circle. Every sharp added changes the key by a fifth. Every flat added changes the key by a fourth.

Each major chord in the Circle of Fifths is shown with its relative minor (on the circle the relative minors are in italics under the major key in this example):

Major Chords:	C	G	D	A	E	B	F♯ /G♭	D♭	A♭	E♭	B♭	F
Relative Minor Chords:	*Am*	*Em*	*Bm*	*F♯m*	*C♯m*	*G♯m*	*D♯m/E♭m*	*B♭m*	*Fm*	*Cm*	*Gm*	*Dm*

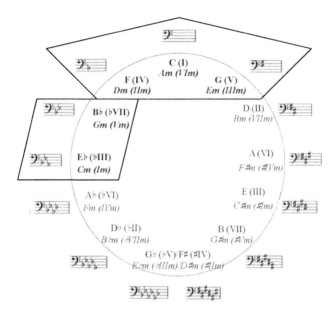

By taking the three chords grouped at the top and their relative minors, we find the six principal chords for that key. In the key of C, the six chords are C/Am, F/Dm, G/Em. The next two positions to the left give the flatted seventh, B♭, and the flatted third, E♭, to complete the Scale of Chords in C:

I	IIm	♭III	IIIm	IV	V	VIm	♭VII
C	Dm	E♭	Em	F	G	Am	B♭

Any place you start on the Circle, the first chord will be the Root (I), the chord to the left will be **IV** and the chord to the right will be **V**. Coupled with the relative minors, it is an easy way of finding the principal chords in any given key. For example, if we start with D, the G to the left is the IV chord, the A to the right is the V chord.

As you can see, this sequence of chords derived from the Circle of Fifths is the same sequence of major and minor chords as derived from the Modes (with the exception of the ♭III and ♭VII).

In most cases, a song will consist of a combination of some of the six principal chords, the I-IIm-IIIm-IV-V-VIm, so when you hear a new song, you can expect to be using a selection of those six chords and their extensions. But songs are not rigidly bound to the conventions of the Circle of Fifths and can go to many surprising places, such as using a major III instead of the IIIm, or a II7 instead of a IIm, or a IVm7 in place of the IV, or some other chord beyond the confines of the Circle to establish a new sound. This is what makes song structure so exciting, there are no strict rules.

You can usually find a Circle of Fifths in a music store, one that can be turned so that the root is in position I and the other chords are given their proper numerical values for that key. Sometimes it is called a *Chord Dial* or a *Wheel of Chords* or a *Transposition Dial.*

The Circle of Fifths and Dominant 7th Chords

In the chapter on *Dominant 7th Chords*, we saw that seventh chords were derived from the Dominant scale, a scale that starts on the 5th of the root scale and uses the same notes as the root scale; for example, the C7 chord is derived from the C Dominant scale of the F major scale.

The Circle of Fifths gives us an easy way to find the root scale of any Dominant scale. Suppose we have a G7 chord and want to know the root scale of G Dominant. If we find G on the Circle and travel counterclockwise one degree, we will come to C. Therefore, C is the root scale of G Dominant.

1	2	3	4	5	6	7	1	2	3	4	5	6	7	1
C	D	E	F	G	A	B	C	D	E	F	G	A	B	C
				1	2	3	4	5	6	7	1			

This works for all Dominant scales, one degree counterclockwise gives the root scale: the root scale of A Dominant is D, the root scale of D Dominant is G, the root scale of C Dominant is F, etc.

Chord Progressions

A **chord progression** is the order of the chords in a song that supports the melody, sometimes also simply called, "the changes." Because melodies and musical phrases usually repeat, the chords are often in a recurring pattern. Once you learn the chord progression for the verse and chorus, the same chords can typically be used for all the verses and chorus repeats for that song. There are some songs in which the melody varies slightly from verse to verse requiring slightly different chord changes.

One of the most common chord progressions in popular music is from the first, to the fourth, to the fifth, and back to the root, I-IV-V-I (in the key of C, that would be from the C to the F to the G, then back to the C). A common variation is I-V-IV-I, from the first to the fifth, then the fourth and return to the root (in C that would be C-G-F-C).

The I-IV-V or I-V-IV three chord progressions are basic progressions and are used in thousands of songs. Even simpler than the three chord progression is the two chord progression, I-IV or I-V. There are many examples of hit songs using just these two or three chord progressions – and many with only one chord, such as Bob Marley's *Exodus.*. So a song does not have to be complicated to be good.

You will find many songs using exactly the same chord progression; this is because a chord progression cannot be copyrighted. A melody or lyric can be copyrighted, but not a chord progression, so the same progressions are used over and over.

Some of the most common chord progressions in major keys are:

- I-V-I
- I-IV-I
- I-V-IV-I (very popular)
- I-IV-V-I (very popular)
- I-IV-I-V-I (a standard Blues progression)
- I-V-VIm-IV (very popular)
- I-V-VIm-IIIm-IV-I-IV-V (Pachelbel's Canon – very popular)
- I-V-IIm-IV (very popular)
- I-VIm-IIm-V (common in jazz)
- I-VIm-IV-V (popular in the 1950s)
- IIm-V-I (common in Jazz)

Here are some popular chord progressions in minor keys:

- Im-Vm
- Im-IVm
- Im-IVm-Vm
- Im-VI-VII
- Im-VII-VI
- Im-III-VII-VI
- Im-VII-IVm-VI
- Im-Vm-VII-IVm
- Im-Vm-IVm-VII
- Im-VII-VI-VII
- Im-VII-VI-V7
- VI-VII-Im

The progressions are shown here in their most basic form; they are often expanded with extended chords, very often with 7th chords. In Blues, for example, there are songs in which all the chords are 7th chords with a progression of I7-IV7-I7-V7-IV7-I7.

Modal Interchange

While the standard chords from the Scale of Chords are often grouped together, in many songs you will encounter chord progressions that stray from the conventional path. You will find ♭III chords substituted for IIIm; minor 7th chords used instead of major chords; and other irregularities. Songwriters are always after new and exciting sounds by expanding the range of chords available and sometimes that means borrowing or substituting chords from other keys.

Borrowing or substituting chords from a parallel major or minor key is called **Modal Interchange**. Borrowed chords are used in a composition in the same way as the common chords of the home key. When there is a complete change to a new key, it is called **Modulation**.

We have already encountered borrowed chords in the chapter on the *Scale of Chords*. The major scale of chords I-IIm-IIIm-IV-V-VIm-VIIm♭5 is often expanded with the addition of a ♭III or ♭VII chords. As the ♭III and ♭VII are not part of the major scale of chords, they are said to be borrowed from the parallel minor.

Major Scale Degrees:	I	IIm	IIIm	IV	V	VIm	VIIm♭5
Chord Scale in C:	C	Dm	Em	F	G	Am	Bm♭5
Chord Scale in Cm:	Cm	Dm♭5	E♭	Fm	Gm	A♭	B♭

Chords can also be borrowed from the parallel major scale for use in the minor scale, for example, using the major V instead of the Vm in a minor key to provide a stronger connection to the I chord is very common.

Secondary Dominant

Chords are often substituted from harmonically related keys. One of the most common substitutions is from the Dominant Scale. In C, the dominant, or fifth, is G.

	I	IIm	IIIm	IV	V	VIm	VIImb5
C Chord Scale:	C	Dm	Em	F	**G**	Am	Bmb5
G Dominant:	G	Am	Bm	C	**D**	Em	F#mb5

The fifth of G is D, so if a D major is used in the key of C in place of a G, it is called a Dominant Substitution or **Secondary Dominant** and written V/V or V7/V. Dominant substitutions are nearly always 7th chords. The dominant of any chord from the IIm to the VIm can be used as a substitute. For example, Dm is the IIm chord of C. The dominant of Dm is A, so an A major can be used as a substitute for the Dm IIm chord. It is noted as V/ii to show that it is the fifth of the IIm chord scale.

	I	IIm	IIIm	IV	V	VIm
Root Scale:	C	Dm	Em	F	G	Am
		V7/ii	V7/iii	V7/IV	V7/V	V7/vi
Secondary Dominant:		A7	B7	C7	D7	E7

The Dominant V chord strongly moves to the Tonic I chord, as we will see in the chapter on *Chord Movement*. Secondary Dominant chords are non-scale chords so they do not resolve to the tonic of the root scale, instead they resolve to the tonic of the scale they are the Dominant of. For example, in the key of C, D7 will resolve to G rather than C; A7 will resolve to Dm; etc. In chord progressions, the secondary dominant is usually followed by the tonic of its own scale, so in C, a D7 will nearly always be followed by a G.

There are many other types of, and reasons for, chord substitutions, but the thing to know is that when a chord appears in a composition that is outside the normal Scale of Chords for the key or strays from the Circle of Fifths, that chord comes from somewhere harmonically related to the root key and is not randomly stuck in. Chord substitutions must always serve the melody in some way.

The ♭VII Chord

We should take a moment to talk about that awkward ♭VII chord. The ♭VII chord is used in many popular songs and common chord progressions, such as I-♭VII-IV-I and I-♭III-♭VII-I. Lennon-McCartney of The Beatles frequently used the ♭VII, as did Jimmy Webb. The chord has also been used in songs by Lynyrd Skynyrd, The Marshall Tucker Band, Pink Floyd, Bob Dylan, ABBA, AC/DC, Alice Cooper, Billy Joel, Boston, Duran Duran, Foo Fighters, Genesis, Jimi Hendrix, Paul Simon, The Rolling Stones, The Who, and many others – it is very common, yet people still seem to have a problem with it.

The ♭VII chord is often used with the other chords in the scale, but it is not a scale chord. The proper chord for the VII position is a VII°, or VIIm♭5, a minor chord with a flat 5, a diminished chord derived from the Locrian mode. However, in popular music, the ♭VII is often used in place of the VII°. The most common explanation for the presence of the ♭VII that it is a borrowed chord from the parallel minor – in the C major scale the 7th note is B, but in the Cm scale, the 7th note is B♭, so when a flat 7 is used in a major scale it is said to be borrowed from the parallel minor.

Major Chord Scale:	I	IIm	IIIm	IV	V	VIm	VII°
C Major:	C	Dm	Em	F	G	Am	Bm♭5
C Minor:	Cm	Dm♭5	E♭	Fm	Gm	A♭	B♭
Minor Scale Degrees:	Im	IIm♭5	III	IVm	Vm	VI	VII

The ♭VII is often used as a substitution for the IV chord and sometimes for the V chord. When substituted for the IV, it is called a "surprise" chord because the ear expects to go to the IV and is surprised when the progression goes to the ♭VII instead. When it follows the IVm7 chord it is called the Backdoor Progression. The ♭VII-V7 cadence was widely used in the early 1960s.

If we turn to the Circle of Fifths we can see one reason why the ♭VII is often used in popular songs instead of the VII°. On the Circle of Fourths, the fourth note of the C scale is F and fourth note of the F scale is B♭, so the B♭ chord is a secondary Subdominant of the Root C chord. The fifth of the scale is called the Dominant, and the fourth of the scale is called the Subdominant; so F is the Subdominant of C, and B♭ is the Subdominant of F, which makes B♭ the secondary-Subdominant of C, written as IV/IV. When the ♭VII is substituted for the F IV chord, it is modal interchange.

Because of its position on the circle, the B♭ becomes the ♭VII of the C Scale of Chords on the Circle of Fifths – there is no diminished chord on the Circle, only the ♭VII.

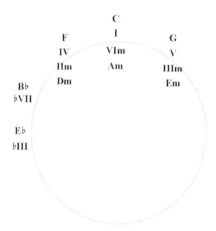

There is one significant change that the ♭VII brings to the Scale of Chords. In a major scale, the 7th note is called the Leading Tone because, only a half-step down from the tonic, it feels like it wants to resolve upwards to the tonic, leading the ear home. The VIImb5 has that leading tone, even though it is a minor chord; however, when we substitute the ♭VII, we lose the leading tone, using the Subtonic instead, a whole step below the tonic, and thus change the function of the chord. The ♭VII still wants to resolve, but not as strongly to the tonic, it can move to other chords besides the I – it is more strongly drawn to the IV chord than it is to the I.

For example, in the C scale, the 7th scale degree, the leading tone, is B. In the C Scale of Chords, the VIIm7♭5 is a Bm7♭5 with the notes B-D-F-A, so the chord contains that critical B leading tone. But when we change to B♭, the ♭VII7, with the notes B♭-D-F-A♭, we lose the B leading tone. Using the ♭VII or ♭VII7 dramatically changes the functional harmony of the chords of the scale and has a dynamic effect on chord progressions and the songs based on them.

Modal Chord Scales

With more modal songs entering popular music, it is helpful to understand modal chord scales. We saw that we can derive a Scale of Chords from the modes starting with C Ionian (C-Dm-Em-F-G-Am-Bmb5) and that if we start our modal series with the Aeolian we can derived the minor scale of chords (Am-Bmb5-C-Dm-Em-F-G).

Similarly, we can derive a scale of chords for each mode. Here is the Dorian scale of chords derived from the modes:

D Dorian (I)

1	2	b3	4	5	6	b7	8							1-b3-5-b7
D	E	F	G	A	B	C	D	E	F	G	A	B	C	D-F-A-C
w	w	h	w	w	w	h	w	w	h	w	w	w	h	Dm7

E Phrygian (II)

	1	b2	b3	4	5	b6	b7	8						1-b3-5-b7
D	E	F	G	A	B	C	D	E	F	G	A	B	C	E-G-B-D
w	w	h	w	w	w	h	w	w	h	w	w	w	h	Em7

F Lydian (bIII)

		1	2	3	#4	5	6	7	8					1-3-5-7
D	E	F	G	A	B	C	D	E	F	G	A	B	C	F-A-C-E
w	w	h	w	w	w	h	w	w	h	w	w	w	h	Fmaj7

G Mixolydian (IV)

			1	2	3	4	5	6	b7	8				1-3-5-b7
D	E	F	G	A	B	C	D	E	F	G	A	B	C	G-B-D-F
w	w	h	w	w	w	h	w	w	h	w	w	w	h	G7

A Aeolian (V)

				1	2	b3	4	5	b6	b7	8			1-b3-5-b7
D	E	F	G	A	B	C	D	E	F	G	A	B	C	A-C-E-G
w	w	h	w	w	w	h	w	w	h	w	w	w	h	Am7

B Locrian (VI)

					1	b2	b3	4	b5	b6	b7	8		1-b3-b5-b7
D	E	F	G	A	B	C	D	E	F	G	A	B	C	B-D-F-A
w	w	h	w	w	w	h	w	w	h	w	w	w	h	Bm7b5

C Ionian (bVII)

						1	2	3	4	5	6	7	8	1-3-5-7
D	E	F	G	A	B	C	D	E	F	G	A	B	C	C-E-G-B
w	w	h	w	w	w	h	w	w	h	w	w	w	h	Cmaj7

If instead of Ionian as our I, we start with Dorian as the I chord, then the II chord is derived from Phrygian mode, the III chord from the Lydian, the IV chord from the Mixolydian, the V chord from the Aeolian, the VI chord from the Locrian and the VII chord from the Ionian.

This gives us a Dorian scale of chords:

Dorian Chord Scale:	Im	IIm	bIII	IV	Vm	VImb5	bVII
D Dorian Chords:	Dm	Em	F	G	Am	Bmb5	C

When we compare the scale degrees of the Dorian mode and the natural minor scale, the Aeolian mode, the only difference between the two modes is the b6:

Dorian Mode Degrees:	1	2	b3	4	5	6	b7
Minor Scale Degrees:	1	2	b3	4	5	b6	b7

But when we compare the scale of chords of the Dorian and the Aeolian, things are very different:

Dorian:	Im	IIm	bIII	IV	Vm	VImb5	bVII
Minor:	Im	IImb5	bIII	IVm	Vm	bVI	bVII

Although both Dorian and Aeolian are minor modes, a song written in the Dorian mode will have a much different emotional tone than a song written in the natural minor scale of chords. Dorian is often used in folk, Latin style music and funk, as well as in jazz numbers such as *So What* by Miles Davis.

We can build a scale of chords for each mode:

	1	2	3	4	5	6	7
Ionian	I	IIm	IIIm	IV	V	VIm	VIImb5
Dorian	Im	IIm	bIII	IV	Vm	VImb5	bVII
Phrygian	Im	bII	bIII	IVm	Vmb5	bVI	bVIIm
Lydian	I	II	IIIm	#IVmb5	V	VIm	VIIm
Mixolydian	I	IIm	IIImb5	IV	Vm	VIm	bVII
Aeolian	Im	IImb5	bIII	IVm	Vm	bVI	bVII
Locrian	Imb5	bII	bIIIm	IVm	bV	bVI	bVIIm

The table above can be used to convert any scale of chords into a parallel mode. For example, to convert C Ionian into C Aeolian:

C Ionian (I)	I	IIm	IIIm	IV	V	VIm	VIImb5
from the C scale	C	Dm	Em	F	G	Am	Bmb5
C Aeolian (VI)	Im	IImb5	bIII	IVm	Vm	bVI	bVII
from the Eb scale	Cm	Dmb5	Eb	Fm	Gm	Ab	Bb

C Aeolian is the relative minor of Eb, so the same chords can be derived as the natural minor scale of chords from Eb, starting on the VI:

	I	IIm	IIIm	IV	V	VIm	VII°	I	IIm	IIIm	IV	V
Chord Scale in Eb:	Eb	Fm	Gm	Ab	Bb	Cm	Dmb5	Eb	Fm	Gm	Ab	Bb
Chord Scale in Cm:	Eb	Fm	Gm	Ab	Bb	Cm	Dmb5	Eb	Fm	Gm	Ab	Bb

150

Chord Function

Understanding how chords relate to the melody gives an introduction to the structure of chord progressions and the structure of songs. Knowing chords, their relationships and their resolutions will help in understanding bass lines. Chords are related to the melody and the bassline moves the accompaniment through the chord progression. Each chord scale degree has a name:

I	Tonic
IIm	Supertonic
IIIm	Mediant
IV	Subdominant
V	Dominant
VIm	Sub-mediant
bVII	Subtonic
VII°	Leading

This gives us three groups of harmoniously related chords: the Tonic Group, consisting of the I, IIIm and VIm; the Subdominant (or Pre-Dominant Group), made up of IIm and IV chords; and the Dominant Group, with the V and VII°. The bVII is not a scale chord, but as the bVII is a secondary subdominant of the IV chord, it is usually included in the Subdominant group.

Group	Chord Degree	Name	Chord (in C)
Tonic Group	I	Tonic	C
	IIIm	Mediant	Em
	VIm	Sub-mediant	Am
Subdominant Group	IV	Subdominant	F
	IIm	Supertonic	Dm
	bVII	Subtonic	Bb
Dominant Group	V	Dominant	G
	VII°	Leading	Bmb5

These groupings are not precise and you will find different variations, but the groupings are useful for understanding the interrelationships of chords. Notice that the I chord and its relative minor the VIm chord are both in the Tonic Group; the IV chord and its relative minor the IIm are both in the Subdominant Group. The V chord is split from its relative minor with the V chord in the Dominant Group while the IIIm relative minor in the Tonic Group.

The chord groups have harmonic function. Although the relationship and movement of chords has to do with shared notes and internal chord structure, harmonic function has more to do with the feeling of music; because of this, chords can have different harmonic functions in different styles of music. Chords of the Tonic Group have Tonic Function, they sound stable, like a home base; the Tonic is usually where a composition begins and/or ends (but not always). Chords of the Dominant Group have Dominant Function, creating a feeling of tension and expectation of a return to the Tonic. The Subdominant chords are transitional chords that want to move, either to build tension or leading to resolving the tension. Seventh chords especially want to move somewhere.

In the chapter on the ♭VII chord we saw how substituting the ♭VII for the VIIm♭5 loses the leading tone and changes the chord functions. Without the leading tone the ♭VII lacks Dominant function. Taking away the VIIm♭5 by substituting the ♭VII leaves only one chord in the Dominant Group, the V; this isn't such a great loss as the VIIm♭5 isn't often used in popular music, although much more common in jazz. An advantage of using the ♭VII is that it adds another transition chord to the Subdominant group, which provides more places to go, facilitating chord movement for more lively progressions.

Chord Function is based on the internal structure of chords, the inter-relationship of the notes of the chords (shown in the table in the key of C with the notes in scale position, not in the order they are normally played in the chords):

			Scale Degrees:	1	2	3	4	5	b6	6	b7	7
			Chord Tones:	C	D	E	F	G	Ab	A	Bb	B
Tonic Group	Imaj7	Cmaj7	C-E-G-B	C		E		G				B
	IIIm7	Em7	E-G-B-D		D	E		G				B
	VIm7	Am7	A-C-E-G	C		E		G		A		
Subdominant Group	IVmaj7	Fmaj7	F-A-C-E	C		E	F			A		
	IIm7	Dm7	D-F-A-C	C	D		F			A		
	bVII7	Bb7	Bb-D-F-Ab		D		F		Ab		Bb	
Dominant Group	V7	G7	G-B-D-F		D		F	G				B
	VII°	Bm7b5	B-D-F-A		D		F			A		B

All the chords in the Tonic Group have the 3rd and 5th of the scale. They form a group because they have common groups of notes. Both the Cmaj7 (Imaj7) and the Am7 (VIm7) share the C-E-G triad and the Cmaj7 (Imaj7) and the Em7 (IIIm7) share the E-G-B triad.

The IV chord straddles the Tonic and Subdominant Groups having the third, but not the fifth. The Fmaj7 (IVmaj7) shares the A-C-E triad with the Am7 (VIm7) of the Tonic Group and shares the F-A-C triad with the Dm7 (IIm7) in the Subdominant Group.

The Subdominant chord group has the 4th and 6th of the scale, which draws them to the Dominant Group, which also has the 4 of the scale as well as the 2. In the Dominant Group, the G7 (V7) and the Bmb5 (VIImb5) share the B-D-F triad. The chords of the Dominant group do not have the tonic, but they do have the seventh leading tone. The absence of the tonic note and presence of the leading tone strongly make the Dominant chords want to resolve to the tonic. (**Note:** this is the 7th note of the *scale*, not the 7 or b7 of the *chord*.)

The bIII, a common borrowed chord in major progressions, is even more difficult to place than the bVII. In the key of C, the bIII is Eb with the notes Eb-G-Bb-Db. It has a G note, the fifth of C, which probably places it in the Tonic Group, although it lacks the major 3rd and the tonic. In the C scale, the Eb is the b3rd, giving the chord a minor function in the scale of chords, even though it is a major chord, so it kind of straddles major and minor, which makes it an interesting chord, but hard to place.

The ear moves easily from one group of tones to another group of tones. The ear is always listening for a resolution to the tonic, from dissonance to harmony. Songwriters introduce dissonance to make the ear listen for a

Content

resolution. The Tonic, or Root, is the starting point, the home tone – all the harmony depends on the root chord.

- The I chord, the Tonic, can move to any other chord in the scale, but is strongly drawn to the V, IV and VIm.
- The IIm chord is the Supertonic; it is most strongly drawn to the V and VII°; rarely goes to the I chord
- The IIIm chord is the Mediant; it is most strongly drawn to the VIm and the IV; rarely goes to the I or VII°.
- The IV chord is the Subdominant; it is most strongly drawn to the I, IIm, V, bVII and VII°.
- The V chord is the Dominant; it is most strongly drawn to the I and the VIm; rarely goes to the IIm or VII°.
- The VIm is the Sub-mediant; it is most strongly drawn to the IIm and IV; rarely goes to the I or VII°,
- The VII° is the Leading chord; it is most strongly drawn to the I and the IIIm; rarely moves to the IIm or IV.
- The bVII is the Subtonic and, in a way, straddles the Dominant and Subdominant groups, which makes it a tension chord that strongly moves towards resolution. It is sometimes used as an alternative to the IV and occasionally the V. The bVII is most strongly drawn to the IV, VIm, bIII and I; it rarely goes to the IIm.

Here are the common chord movements in table form:

		Goes to:								
		Most often		Less often		Sometimes			Rarely	
Tonic	I	V	IV		VIm	IIm	IIIm	bVII		
	IIIm	VIm		IV		IIm	V		I	VII°
	VIm	IV	IIm	IIIm	V			bVII	I	VII°
Subdominant	IIm	V	VII°	IV	VIm		IIIm		I	
	IV	V	I	IIm	bVII	VIm	IIIm	VII°		
	bVII	IV		I	VIm		bIII		IIm	
Dominant	V	I		IV	VIm		IIIm		IIm	VII°
	VII°	I	IIIm		V	VIm			IIm	IV

We can see from some common chord progressions how the chord groups relate to each other. Under the chord progression are their groups (in brackets).

- I-IV-V-I

  I (Tonic) → **IV** (Subdominant) → **V** (Dominant) → **I** (Tonic)
- I-V-VIm-IV

  I (Tonic) → **V** (Dominant) → **VIm** (Tonic) → **IV** (Subdominant)
- I-V-IIm-IV

  I (Tonic) → **V** (Dominant) → **IIm** (Tonic) → **IV** (Subdominant)
- I-VIm-IIm-V

  I (Tonic) → **VIm** (Tonic) → **IIm** (Subdominant) → **V** (Dominant)
- I-VIm-IV-V

  I (Tonic) → **VIm** (Tonic) → **IV** (Subdominant) → **V** (Dominant)

The chord progressions keep moving through the three groups of chords, building and resolving tension. Where there are more than two chords, the progressions always use chords from all three groups. This is how chord progressions are structured and is basic to understanding songs.

The chords don't normally progress to a chord within the same group, although I-VIm, both in the Tonic group, is a popular progression. Starting a new section of a song, such as the bridge, on the VIm is quite common (see the chapter on the *Bridge* in the *Song Structure* section). Notice that none of the most common chord progressions listed above use the IIIm, the ♭III, the ♭VII or the VII°, but there are songs that use these chords.

Tonics move to Subdominants which move to Dominants which move to Tonics. The Tonic is a stable chord, it naturally goes to a Subdominant chord. The Subdominants are called moving chords because they want to go somewhere. Using Subdominants builds anticipation in the listener and moves the melody forward. The Subdominant moves to a Dominant, which introduces an expectation of resolution when the Dominant returns to the Tonic. You can see why certain chord progressions are so popular and are used in so many catchy songs – they take advantage of the strongest harmonic relationships between chords.

Basically, what a chord progression is trying to do is go somewhere and then return to the tonic in the strongest or most interesting way.

These chord movements can be altered by chord extensions. The most common extension is the Dominant 7th. The Dominant 7th introduces a discordance that seeks resolution usually by moving down a fifth or up a fourth.

The chord relationships also hold true for the minor keys, which makes sense as the minor keys are relative minors of the major keys. But there is one exception: the strongest approach to the III chord is the VII, a major chord, not the VII° as in the major keys. In minor keys, the V chord is very often played as a major chord instead of a minor chord to increase the Dominant Function leading to the Tonic.

ii-V-I

The ii-V-I is a common chord progression, especially in jazz. To understand it, let's start with the scale of chords in C:

I	IIm	IIIm	IV	V	VIm	VIImb5
C	Dm	Em	F	G	Am	Bmb5

Now let's look at the Circle of Fifths:

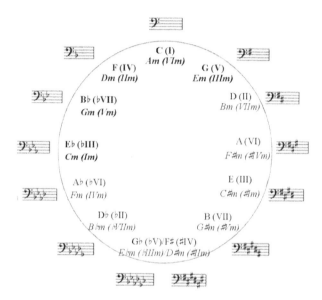

We can create a chord progression by going around the circle. If we start on D and go counterclockwise, the next chord will be G, and the next chord C.

If we are in the key of C, we know that the II chord is minor, so our starting chord, D, is going to be Dm, the IIm of C. The next chord is G, which is the V chord of C, and finally the I chord of the key of C is C. Moving counterclockwise around the Circle of Fifths gives us our ii-V-I progression. The ii-V-I is a progression of descending fifths as D is the fifth of G and G is the fifth of C. In the key of C, D is the dominant of G and therefore, D is the secondary dominant of C.

From D to G to C is traveling around the circle counterclockwise, the Circle of Fourths, where G is the fourth of D and C is the fourth of G, so why are we descending in fifths and not in fourths? It would be in fourths if we were in the key of D. In the key of D, to move from D (I) to G (IV) to C (♭VII) counter-clockwise around the circle is to move in fourths. But we are in the key of C with C as I chord. In C, their position on the circle makes G the fifth of C and D the fifth of G, so we are descending in fifths from D, the fifth of G, to G, the fifth of C, to the I chord, C.

It depends on how we count. If we start on D and move in fourths we get D-G-C:

1	2	3	4	5	6	7	1			
D	E	F♯	G	A	B	C♯	D			
			1	2	3	4	5	6	7	1
			G	A	B	C	D	E	F♯	G

But when we are in the key of C, the tones are a fifth apart:

Ascending 5th →										
1	2	3	4	5	6	7	1			
C	D	E	F	G	A	B	C			
5	4	3	2	1						
← Descending 5th										
			Ascending 5th →							
			1	2	3	4	5	6	7	1
			G	A	B	C	D	E	F♯	G
			5	4	3	2	1			
			← Descending 5th							

···so beginning on D, we descend in fifths D-G-C to C.

Using the Dm involves Modal Interchange. There is no Dm chord in the G scale of chords, but there is a Dm in the Gm scale of chords. In the key of Gm, the fifth chord is Dm, so when used in the G major scale of chords, the Dm is borrowed from the Gm scale and becomes a minor secondary dominant, the IIm of the C scale.

The ii-V-I progression moves through all three chord groups; the IIm is in the Subdominant Group, the V is Dominant and the I is Tonic.

The table of chord movements shows us that the IIm strongly moves to the V and the V strongly moves to the I, so the progression takes advantage of some of the strongest chord associations in the scale.

	Most often goes to:
IIm	V
V	I
I	V

The ii-V-I is nearly always played with extensions to expand the range of the chords, often as 7th chords: ii7-V7-Imaj7, although also with 9 and 13 tensions and alterations.

The ii-V-I can be played in a minor form as well. The Vm of the minor scale lacks the strong pull to the tonic as the V major, so the V chord is played as a major rather than a minor. In the minor scale the II chord is diminished and the I chord is minor giving us Dm7♭5-G7-Cm7.

Transposing

Transposing is modulating a song from one key to another. The chords of any key correspond to different chords in the same position in any other key – at least in position, not always in emotional tone, brightness, pathos or pleasantness. The Scale of Chords pattern from the Circle of Fifths is the same for every major key:

Scale of Chord Degrees:	I	IIm	♭III	IIIm	IV	V	VIm	♭VII	VIIm♭5

Suppose you have a song that uses the chords C, F and G, but the singer wants it in E to better suit her voice. What do you do? You use the Circle of Fifths to transpose to the new key. There are transposition dials that have two turnable circles; you set the first one to the original key, then set the second to the new key and play the corresponding chords.

Chord Table:

Major / Minor	I	IIm	♭III	IIIm	IV	V	VIm	♭VII	VIIm♭5
C / Am	C	Dm	E♭	Em	F	G	Am	B♭	Bm♭5
D♭ / B♭m	D♭	E♭m	E	Fm	G♭	A♭	B♭m	B	Cm♭5
D / Bm	D	Em	F	F♯m	G	A	Bm	C	C♯m♭5
E♭ / Cm	E♭	Fm	G♭	Gm	A♭	B♭	Cm	D♭	Dm♭5
E / C♯m	E	F♯m	G	G♯m	A	B	C♯m	D	D♯m♭5
F / Dm	F	Gm	A♭	Am	B♭	C	Dm	E♭	Em♭5
F♯ / D♯m	F♯	G♯m	A	A♯m	B	C♯	D♯m	E	Fm♭5
G♭ / E♭m	G♭	A♭m	A	B♭m	B	D♭	E♭m	E	Fm♭5
G / Em	G	Am	B♭	Bm	C	D	Em	F	F♯m♭5
A♭ / Fm	A	B♭m	B	Cm	D♭	E♭	Fm	G♭	Gm♭5
A / F♯m	A	Bm	C	C♯m	D	E	F♯m	G	G♯m♭5
B♭ / Gm	B♭	Cm	D♭	Dm	E♭	F	Gm	A♭	Am♭5
B / G♯m	B	C♯m	D	D♯m	E	F♯	G♯m	A	A♯m♭5

F♯ and G♭ are enharmonic

So, our problem is that we have a C-F-G chord progression and we want to play it in the key of E. In the key of C, C-F-G are the I-IV-V chords. If we search down the table to E, we see that the I-IV-V chords in E are E-A-B. If we play E-A-B, we have transposed C-F-G to the new key.

	I	IIm	♭III	IIIm	IV	V	VIm	♭VII	VIIm♭5
C	C	Dm	E♭	Em	F	G	Am	B♭	Bm♭5
E	E	F♯m	G	G♯m	A	B	C♯m	D	D♯m♭5

If we wanted the song in B♭, we would have B♭-E♭-F; in G it would be G-C-D. In each case we are keeping the chords in the same progression, I-IV-V, but using the chords that correspond to those chord degrees in each key.

In order to transpose keys, first translate the chords into degrees of the Scale of Chords using Roman Numeral Analysis, such as I-VIm-IIm-V, then find those degrees in the same order in the new key. I-VIm-IIm-V in C would be C-Am-Dm-G. Transpose that same progression, I-VIm-IIm-V, into the key of A and we have, A-F♯m-Bm-E. If there are 7th chords in the original key, there will be 7th chords in the new key as well (this is true for all chord extensions). A Blues progression of I7-IV7-I7-V7-I7 in C would be C7-F7-C7-G7-C7; in E♭ it would be E♭7-A♭7- E♭7-B♭7- E♭7.

The same procedure works for the minor scales as well.

Key Changes

Key changes, also called **Modulation**, or the Transition, can occur within a song or in a medley of several songs joined together. Sometimes it is possible to jump directly from one key to another, called Direct Modulation, but often a little adjustment is required so the ear accepts the change in tonal range easily without being jarred. The chords used to accomplish a key change are called transition chords or pivot chords. Sometimes only one pivot chord is required, but sometimes a short chord progression is needed.

There are a number of ways to achieve smooth key changes with chords and chord progressions. One way is to find the V7 chord of the new key. To transition from C to F, for example, the V7 of F is C7, so a songwriter or arranger would play C, then C7 and then enter the chord progression for F. To transition from C to G, the V7 of G is D7, so an arrangement might go directly from C to the D7 to enter the key of G. As D major is the fifth of G, and G is the fifth of C, using the D major in C is the secondary dominant, called the five of five, or V/V.

The composer might also go to the IIm7 of C, Dm7, then to the D7 and from there into the key of G. Both Dm7 and D7 have the same ♭7.

Another approach uses shared chords. Suppose a song modulates from C major to G major.

	I	IIm	♭III	IIIm	IV	V	VIm	♭VII
C Major:	C	Dm	E♭	Em	F	G	Am	B♭
G Major:	G	Am	B♭	Bm	C	D	Em	F

In the Scale of Chords, the keys of C and G share the chords C, Em, G and Am (as well as B♭ as optional ♭III and ♭VII chords). Any of these chords could be used as an entry to the new key. Often the IV and IIm7 are used as pivot chords because they are moving chords of the Subdominant group and so lead to ear to listen for a resolution, usually moving to a chord in the Dominant group and then to the Tonic group.

Keys such as E and F don't have any common chords.

	I	IIm	♭III	IIIm	IV	V	VIm	♭VII
E Major:	E	F♯m	G	G♯	A	B	C♯m	D
F Major:	F	Gm	A♭	Am	B♭	C	Dm	E♭

It's only one half-step up, so the arrangement could easily go directly to the new key, or you might find that the composer will go to the IV in E, which is A, then modify to A7, then go to Am or Am7, which is the IIIm or IIIm7 of F, and enter the new key.

Seventh chords, augmented chords and diminished seventh chords can be used for smooth key transitions because they often have shared notes. For example, Caug, Eaug and G♯aug all use the notes C-E-G♯. Because the chord is common to all three keys (even though it has a different name and note order in each key) it can be used as a pivot and resolve to the IV or VIm of the new key, provided it works with the melody.

	1	3	5♯
Caug	C	E	G♯
Eaug	E	G♯	C
G♯aug	G♯	C	E

Diminished seventh chords can resolve in a number of ways, which makes them useful for modulation, but their use is somewhat hampered by their harsh sound. Diminished seventh chords share notes in a number of keys.

The table shows the diminished chords that share notes (the shared chords are grouped together; enharmonic keys shown with a [bracket):

		1	b3	b5	bb7
	Cdim7	C	Eb	Gb	Bbb (A)
[	D#dim7	D# (Eb)	F# (Gb)	A	C
	Ebdim7	Eb	Gb	Bbb (A)	Dbb (C)
[	F#dim	F# (Gb)	A	C	D# (Eb)
	Gbdim7	Gb	Bbb (A)	Dbb (C)	Fbb (Eb)
	Adim7	A	C	Eb	Gb
	Bdim7	B	D	F	Ab
	Ddim7	D	F	Ab	Cb (B)
[	G#dim7	G# (Ab)	B	D	F
	Abdim7	Ab	Cb (B)	Ebb (D)	Gbb (F)
	Fdim7	F	Ab	Cb (B)	Ebb (D)
[	A#dim7	A# (Bb)	C# (Db)	E	G
	Bbdim7	Bb	Db	Fb (E)	Abb (G)
[	C#dim7	C# (Db)	E	G	A# (Bb)
	Dbdim7	Db	Fb (E)	Abb (G)	Cbb (Bb)
	Edim7	E	G	Bb	Db
	Gdim7	G	Bb	Db	Fb (E)

Key changes in popular music are usually between neighboring keys. For example, in *Me and Bobby McGee* by Kris Kristofferson, the key steps up from G to A after the first chorus. Barry Manilow was known for raising the final chorus of his songs a half-step to give the ending a little positive sounding lift. In popular music this is called a step-up or pump-up; in country music it is sometimes called a gear change or a truck-driver's change.

Sometimes the instrumental section is in a different key than the verse/chorus, and sometimes the bridge will go to a new key. You may run into a situation where a singer wants a number in one key because of vocal range and the lead guitarist wants it in another key because the solo he or she has worked out relies heavily on using open strings and it can't be transposed without losing the effect. This will require a transition to the new key for the solo, then back to the home key for the singer.

Chords and Melody

We know that songs are built on the Scale of Chords and that chords support the melody, so, what is the relationship between the chords and the melody? A basic chord consists of three harmonious tones, the 1-3-5 triad of the scale. The chords used in a song are those with tones that best harmonize with the melody notes. Designating the chords of a song is called harmonizing the melody or harmonization.

When playing chords we aren't playing melody, we are playing harmony. Understanding how the melody relates to the chords is an introduction to how the bassline relates to the chords.

Let's look at a simple example, *Twinkle Twinkle Little Star*, just the first four bars (you don't have to be able to read sheet music to understand this, it will give you a visual sense of relationship of chords to melody) – because it is a melody it is shown here in the treble staff rather than the bass staff:

The song is in the key of C and the chords are C, F, G (they written along the top of the staff) – the I-IV-V of the C Scale of Chords. All the chords are major chords, there are no minor chords, seventh chords or other chord variations. The chord progression is I-IV-I-IV-I-V-I. Even a simple song like *Twinkle Twinkle Little Star* uses chords from all three chord groups:

I (Tonic) → IV (Subdominant) → I (Tonic) → IV (Subdominant) → I (Tonic) → V (Dominant) → I (Tonic)

Now let's look as the notes of the song (note names are written below the staff):

In Scale Degrees of the C major scale, the melody goes:

C	C	G	G	A	A	G	F	F	E	E	D	D	C
1	1	5	5	6	6	5	4	4	3	3	2	2	1

As you can see, the last two bars are a simple walk-down of the scale: 4-3-2-1.

These are all notes of the C major scale. We find the melody notes C, F and G, which correspond to the C-F-G chords, but we also have A and E notes. Why don't we have A and E chords?

Let's ghost in the chord tones over the melody:

Chord:	C			F	C	F		C		G		C
Melody Note:	C	C	G	G	A	A	G	F	F	E	E	D	D	C
Note Degree:	1	1	5	5	6	6	5	4	4	3	3	2	2	1

Twin-kle twin-kle lit-tle star, how I won-der what you are.

The melody starts on a C note with a C chord; that seems straight forward enough. The next note is a G. For every note in a melody there are three chords in the Scale of Chords that will harmonize with that note. To find the chords, start with the chord with the target note as the root, then count down in thirds. For the G note, start with the G chord then count down a third to the Em, then down a third to C.

Degree:	I	IIm	IIIm	IV	V	VIm	VIImb5
Chords:	C	Dm	Em	F	G	Am	Bmb5
Fifth	G	A	B	C	D	E	F
Third	E	F	G	A	B	C	D
Root	C	D	E	F	G	A	B

The chord tones of the C chord are C-E-G, so the G is another chord tone of C and is covered by the C chord. The G is the Dominant Fifth of the C scale and so is harmonically tied to the tonic – our old friends the root and fifth.

The next note is an A. The A requires a chord change because there is no A tone in a C chord (C-E-G). So we move from the C to an F chord (F-A-C). Why not an A chord?

Of the C-scale chords that have an A note, we have Am (A-C-E), F (F-A-C) or Dm (D-F-A). We want our chords to move through the different chord groups. The VIm is in the Tonic group, the same as our starting I chord, so the Am is not our preferred movement. Both the IV and the IIm are in the Subdominant group, which is where we want to move to, but the IIm would introduce a minor tonality, which would dramatically change the emotional feel of the song to something much more somber. The F major (F-A-C), IV chord sounds most harmonious and brightest – it is our safest choice. F is the Perfect Fourth of the C scale and is harmonically tied to the tonic.

We have moved from the Tonic to the Subdominant, then we have another G note, again covered by a C chord (Tonic group); then two F notes covered by an F chord (Subdominant group).

Next we have two E notes, again covered by a C chord (Tonic group). Why not an E chord? The available chords in C with an E note are Em (IIIm), C (I) and Am (VI). We want to move to the Tonic Group, so that eliminates Em. Of the Tonic chords, the Am would add a minor tone, which we don't want in this accompaniment, so the C major is the safest chord.

Next are two D notes covered by a G (G-B-D) V chord. The V is strongly drawn to the I so using it takes advantage of a strong harmonic relationship. (In the illustration, the D note in the sheet music is actually the octave D of the G chord shown on the staff.) Notice that the G notes in the first and second bars are covered by C chords, while the G chord in the fourth bar is used to cover the D notes.

At the end of the fourth bar, the melody resolves to the tonic C.

This example shows how the chords pick up the melody tones. The melody note does not have to be the root of the chord, it can be the third, the fifth, or an extension tone. Of course, melodies are not restricted to chord tones, they nearly always encompass non-chord tones, which can also be covered by chords and their extensions.

Melodies do not have to start on the root note of the initial chord, they can also start on the third or fifth of the chord. In C, the melody can begin with C or E or G.

Because the same notes are used in different chords, there is a great deal of variation in chord transcription for the same melody because the person transcribing was picking up different melody tones and/or using different chords to represent the melody tones. There is never only one way to harmonize a chord progression to a melody – none of them are wrong, they are simply different.

Chord changes in songs usually fall on the accented beats of the melody. In *Twinkle Twinkle Little Star*, in 4/4 time, the accents are on the first and third beats of the four beat bar (strong on the first, not as strong on the third):

Twin-kle **twin**-kle | **lit**-tle **sta**-ar | **how** I **won**-der | **what** you **ar**-re.

Changing chords on the accents isn't a strict rule as chords can change anywhere the melody demands, but it is true for much popular music. Singers often change the accent beat to suit their phrasing, so the chord changes do not always follow the accents.

In many arrangements you will find extra chords that are not based on melody notes, but are there to add color, dynamics, harmony, provide leading tones to the next chord, or to build tension.

Chords and Basslines

We saw in the chapter on *Chords and Melody* how the 1st-3rd-5th chord tones picked up the melody notes. Vocal harmony typically targets the 3rd and 6th above or below the melody. A bassline can harmonize with both the melody and the chords giving us the target notes of 1st-3rd-5th-6th-8th. Here's a bassline to look at:

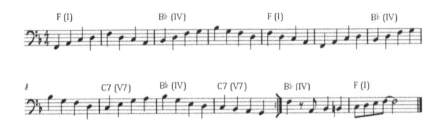

First, let's look at the chords. It's a quick change blues in F major using I-IV-V. If we look at the chord movement we can see that the chords move through all the three groups:

I (Tonic) → **IV** (Subdominant) → I (Tonic) → **IV** (Subdominant) → **V7** (Dominant) → **IV** (Subdominant) → **V7** (Dominant) → **IV** (Subdominant) → I (Tonic).

The notes available for each chord are:

	1	2	3	4	5	6	b7	7	8	
F	F	G	A	Bb	C	D	Eb	E	F	F-A-C
Bb	Bb	C	D	Eb	F	G	Ab	A	Bb	Bb-D-F
C7	C7	D	E	F	G	A	Bb	B	C	C-E-G-Bb

Here are the notes with the scale degrees relative to the chords written underneath:

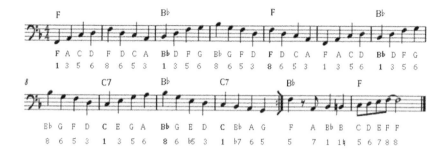

We saw that the target notes for basslines were 1st-3rd-5th-6th-8th – and that is exactly the series of notes we find in this line, with some slight variations. Nearly all the movement in this bassline is in the Imperfect Consonance of thirds, both major and minor, interspersed with the dissonant major second.

The 1st-3rd-5th-6th-8th are found in the major pentatonic scale for the F and Bb chords.

	1	2	3	5	6	8
F Pentatonic:	F	G	A	C	D	F
Bb Pentatonic:	Bb	C	D	F	G	Bb

The C7 chord relies on the Mixolydian mode with the flat seven. In bar 10, the Bb chord uses the E as a b5 blue note as a passing tone to walk down in minor thirds. The bassline is always moving towards the root or octave of the next chord.

Of course, bass lines are not limited to the 1st-3rd-5th-6th-8th of the scale, they are simply common target harmony notes. Things very quickly get much more complex, but this illustrates a basic harmony approach to basslines. The target notes will change depending on the chord progression and the song. For some arrangements, targeting the 3rd-5th-b7^{th} may be the best approach.

There is much more to a memorable bassline than notes, intervals and harmony. A bassline also has emotional content, a feel or mood that complements the melody. The low vibrations of the bass are felt as well as heard. Some of the principles from Baroque *basso continuo* (figured bass) are still relevant to basslines today: the accompaniment should not be too strong or too weak; it should support the other voices; and should not disturb, confuse or overshadow with excessive ornamentation.

Song Structure

We have seen how the chords from which songs are constructed relate to each other through Scales, the Scale of Chords, the Circle of Fifths and chord progressions. Now we can go on to look at the various elements that make up a song.

There is no such thing as "standard" or "normal" song structure. Every song has unique elements. Part of a bass player's job, and part of the fun of playing bass, is to bring out the uniqueness in every song.

There is no strict nomenclature for the component parts of songs, different terms mean different things to different people at different places at different times, so if someone says a Break is a pause in the middle of a song and someone else says a Break is an instrumental solo in a song, they are both right.

Although there is no common structure to songs, there are common elements (*note*: this list is not exhaustive; you will find other song elements in your experience as a musician):

1. Melody
2. Lyrics
3. Arrangement
4. The Build: Tension and Resolution
5. Call and response
6. Intro
7. Lead in
8. Verse
9. Pre-chorus
10. Chorus
11. Tag-line or Refrain
12. Hook
13. Turnaround
14. Break
15. Bridge or middle-eight
16. Solo section
17. Transition
18. Ending, outro or coda
19. Time

21. Beat
22. Tempo
23. Rhythm and groove

These elements can be combined in endless variations. You may never find a song with all of these components, but every song uses some. Many popular songs follow some variation of the verse-chorus-verse-chorus-bridge-chorus form. Each part within a song has its own musical needs.

Melody

Melody is the tune you sing in the shower or hum while driving the car. Melodies can be complex, soaring achievements or simple drones rarely moving from one note. For most songs, the melody is what is most memorable. The melody is a series of notes and those notes are accompanied by a series of chords. The melody is supported by the rhythm and the beat or groove.

Lyrics

The Lyrics are the words of a song sung to the melody. The importance of the lyrics varies from song to song and from music style to music style. Some styles of music, country and folk for example, are lyric-centered – the story of the song is often what is most important; in other styles the lyrics are intentionally distorted and can't be understood. In the best songs, the lyric and the melody complement each other. An example would be *Somewhere over the Rainbow*. The first two notes of the melody jump a full octave, giving a musical experience of flying over the rainbow, as described in the lyrics.

Most song lyrics rhyme, but there are many songs with non-rhyming lyrics as well. Some songwriters insist that each beat should have one syllable, think "Twin-kle twin-kle." Other songwriters will let the words flow over and through the beat, squeezing in many more syllables than there are beats in a bar. Sometimes a single syllable will be stretched over a number of beats (this is usually a vowel sound as it is difficult to sustain consonant sounds).

Arrangement

With songs we are often talking about two separate yet interrelated elements. The song itself is the melody and lyrics. Built around the melody and lyrics is the musical arrangement. Nothing affects the delivery of a song more than the arrangement. If you listen to the same song performed by different artists, you can immediately hear how much the accompaniment affects the presentation of a song. A dynamic arrangement and delivery can greatly enhance a song. For example, the original acoustic release of Simon & Garfunkel's *The Sound of Silence* failed to chart, but when it was remixed with a backing band, it hit number one.

In many contemporary songs, the musical accompaniment is an integral part of the song. Led Zeppelin's *Stairway to Heaven* is defined by the acoustic guitar opening. There are many tunes that are instantly recognizable from the first few instrumental bars, before the melody and lyrics come in. The bass and drum intro from *Another One Bites the Dust* by Queen is immediately recognizable – and unforgettable.

The key and tempo of a song are part of the arrangement. The parts of a song are mostly within the same key and the same tempo, but not always. Key changes can occur within a song and are one way to keep the ears interested. An accompaniment can be stepped up a key so that the ear responds to the new and brighter sound.

Similarly, tempo changes keep the ear engaged. Sometimes the instrumental solo section of a song arrangement will be in a different key and tempo from the verse.

The Build: Tension and Release

In the arrangement, the song usually builds to a climax, often a frenzied chorus or an instrumental solo. The build is important to keep the audience listening. As the song builds it creates tension and anticipation in the audience. They will keep listening for the resolution.

Different chord progressions built tension in different ways. A simple example of tension/resolution is in the major scale. Sing *do-re-mi-fa-so-la-ti-* and the ear wants to hear that final '*do*' – it wants the tension created by the rising scale to be resolved by a return to the tonic. This is the power of tension and resolution in an arrangement. You can guide the ear to a place of expectation, then either provide the solution or maintain the tension by denying the resolution.

There are often dynamics within a song, alternating loud and soft parts, perhaps reducing the accompaniment to one acoustic guitar before bringing the full band back in. The dynamics keep the song interesting and complement the emotional power of the melody and lyrics. The bassline plays a large part in the dynamics of an arrangement.

Call and Response

Call and Response is a type of arrangement in which a musical phrase, either instrumental or vocal, is answered by another musical phrase. It is often used in groups with back-up singers where the lead singer will sing a line and the back-up singers will answer in harmony. Examples of call and response can be found in the Beatles' version of *Twist and Shout* or in *My Generation* by The Who in which the lead singer's lines are supported by the back-up vocals.

Call and Response is also used in instrumental sections where two instruments will alternate phrases, each building on the other. In another form of call and response, you may occasionally hear lyrics punctuated by a couple of instrumental bars.

Call and Response is the basic format of Blues, where the first lines pose a question or set up a situation and the last lines provide and answer or solution to the problem.

Lead in / Pick-up

A lead in, or pick-up, is a short intro, usually of one bar, before starting the melody proper; something like, "Baby I | Want you···" with the song starting on the downbeat of the first bar with "Want you," but with the "Baby I" preceding it.

Intro

The Intro is a musical lead-in, sometimes with lyrics, but usually instrumental, before the main melody. There is a lot of variation with Intros. Sometimes they use a variation of the main melody, but they can also have a completely different melody, key and rhythm from the song proper. Some songs with immediately recognizable intros are *La Grange* by ZZ Top, *Leyla* by Eric Clapton, and *Stairway to Heaven* by Led Zeppelin, to name just a few.

Verse

A verse is a repeated melody with different words, or lyrics, for each repetition. The simplest songs are verse-verse-verse until the end, a form called the Ballad. Ballads are story songs and the story being related in the lyrics is sometimes more important than the musicality. There are various ways to spice up a ballad so that it doesn't devolve into a monotonous drone, such as adding tag lines. Most popular songs alternate verses with a chorus.

Tag Line or Refrain

Instead of a chorus, some songs have a tag line, or refrain. Usually, this is the last line of the verse. The lyrics of the verse change with each repetition of the melody, but the last line remains the same for each repetition. The tag line can also be part of the chorus. The tag line is often the title of the song. An example is Paul Simon's *Sounds of Silence*, in which every verse ends with a variation of the tag phrase, "sounds of silence" or Bob Dylan's *Blowin' in the Wind*, a song in ballad form with no chorus or bridge, but the tag line "blowin' in the wind" at the end of each verse.

Pre-Chorus

The Pre-Chorus is a musical transition between the verse and the chorus. If, for example, the verse ends on the root I and the chorus starts on the IV, the song may use a walk-up, I-IIm-IIIm-IV, to get to the starting chord of the chorus

176

instead of jumping straight to the IV. Not all songs have a pre-chorus, most simply move melodically from the verse to the chorus. Occasionally the pre-chorus will have its own lyrics to lead into the chorus.

Sometimes the pre-chorus can be as simple as having all the instruments stop at the end of the verse and the drummer giving a lead-in to the chorus. The Beatles use this technique in *Lucy in the Sky with Diamonds*.

Chorus

The repetitive verse-verse of a ballad is often varied by the addition of a Chorus. A chorus is a repeating section placed between the verses; it has a different, although usually complementary, melodic line than the verse, but has the same lyrics for each repetition. The different melodic line adds variety. The chorus is often catchy and singable. With many contemporary pop songs, the catchy chorus is the main part of the song and the verses serve mainly to build up to each repetition of the chorus.

A common song order is verse-chorus, but the song can also open with the chorus as in The Beatles' *She Loves You.*

Hook

The Hook is a musical or lyrical phrase that grabs the attention of the audience, usually at the beginning of a verse or a chorus. If the hook has lyrics, it can be called a tag line or refrain. An example would be *Bee-Bop-A-Lula* by Gene Vincent, *Hanky Panky* by Tommy James and the Shondells, or *You Can't Always Get What You Want* by the Rolling Stones.

Turnaround

A Turnaround is a musical phrase used to get from the final note of a verse or chorus to the starting note of the next verse. Most often used in blues or jazz as a set up for the next verse.

Break

A Break is a pause in the middle of a song for dramatic effect. It is often used immediately before or after the musical climax of the song. Usually there is a beat of silence, then a lead in with a fill by the drummer or the band leader counting in *1, 2, 3, 4 ···* to the next section.

Sometimes the break is a I7 or V7 chord after the verse or chorus to set up the bridge. Break can also mean the solo section of an arrangement.

Bridge

A Bridge, or Middle-Eight, is a musical break within a song to give the ear a rest from the repetitive verse-chorus. A bridge can add suspense and drama to a song. The bridge has a different melody than either the verse or chorus, usually a simple variation of the principal melodic line. Bridges start on a different chord than either the verse or the chorus. The IV, the IIIm and VIm are common places to go for the bridge, but they can start anywhere that has a different sound than the verse or chorus. A popular song in a major key might start the bridge on the VIm and shift into the relative minor.

The bridge was originally an eight-bar instrumental interlude in the middle of the song, hence the term Middle-Eight, but later lyrics were added. There are musicians who make a distinction between the bridge, which has lyrics, and the middle-eight, which is purely instrumental.

Over time, the bridge became an integral part of the emotional expression of the song. For example, if a song in a major key goes to the minor third on the bridge, it will provide an opportunity to bring in a more minor emotional tone, bringing more depth to the song. The bridge will sometimes be in a different key than the verse/chorus to add some variety to the song.

You can hear the bridge in a song like, *Somewhere Over the Rainbow*. The first two verses, start with the tag line, "Somewhere, over the rainbow···", then the song moves to the bridge with, "Someday I'll wish upon a star···", then returns to the third verse starting again with the tag line, "Somewhere, over the rainbow···"

Solo-Section

This is a part of the musical arrangement dedicated to a solo instrument or instruments; in popular music that usually means an electric guitar. The solo section can also be called a Break, or if several instruments take solo parts, a Breakdown. What happens here depends on the soloist. The Bridge is written by the composer, but the solo-section is created by the musician. The solo-section can be a musical improvisation over the chord progression of the verse or chorus, or it can be a separate section with its own chord progression, tempo or key. For example, in The Allman Brothers Band live rendition of T-Bone Walker's (*They Call It*) *Stormy Monday*, the section with the keyboard solo is played with a much faster tempo than the moderate blues of the verses.

In performed jazz, the usual presentation is to play the melody, called the head, then each instrument in turn plays a solo of variations on the melody before the band returns to the head.

Transition

A transition is used when there is a key change within a song or in medleys when several songs in different keys are strung together. Changing keys in a song or medley is called Modulation. If the new key is closely related to the root key there will often be a direct movement to the new key, but sometimes the transition involves a short progression of chords that walk up or down to the new key. Seventh chords, augmented chords and diminished chords are often used as transition chords, also called pivot chords.

Ending, Outro, Coda or Tag

The ending is an important part of the arrangement and an exciting ending can fire the audience's desire to hear more. A song that fizzles out inconclusively will leave the audience confused or indifferent. An ending can be anything from a single sustained chord to a complicated progression. What's important is that the tension of the melody is resolved so that the ear is satisfied with a feeling that the song is complete.

Coda is the musical term for the end section of a musical arrangement. A Tag is a conventional ending, the kind often used in blues or folk music. An Outro is a concluding musical section that may include some solo licks by the lead guitarist. An example of a long outro is the "na-na-na" final section of *Hey Jude* by the Beatles.

An ending may involve a cadence, a two chord progression, as a way of completing the final musical phrase. If a song ends with a progression from a V to the I, it is called a perfect cadence. A plagal cadence is from the IV to the I, also called the Church cadence, which you will recognize if you have ever heard a hymn end, *A-men*. There are a great many terms used to describe cadences: authentic, perfect, imperfect, deceptive, evaded and half-cadence, which are all different ways of concluding a piece of music.

Although a cadence is often used at the end a piece, cadences can be used within a composition to end musical phrases.

The following table shows the most common cadences, although technically there are sometimes other requirements to be met, such as the correct inversion of the chords and the position of the tonic of the scale in the cadence, but this will serve as a general guide:

Half-cadence:	any chord	to	V
Authentic cadence:	V or VII°	to	I
Authentic perfect cadence:	V	to	I
Authentic imperfect cadence:	VII°	to	I
Plagal cadence:	IV	to	I
Deceptive or Interrupted cadence*:	V	to	VIm

* the deceptive cadence is commonly to the VIm, but can be to any chord other than the I.

Recorded tracks sometimes fade out rather than come to a conclusive ending, so a performing band may have to come up with their own dynamic ending for a number.

Time / Meter

Time in music is also called meter. The time signature, how many beats per bar, or measure, on the musical staff, has a huge effect on the emotional range of a song. The time of a song is based on a number of notes grouped around an accent beat or beats, called a bar. 4/4 time is the most common time in popular music, in fact it is called "common time." What this means is that if you count 1-2-3-4 with the accent on the '1', then repeat 1-2-3-4, you are counting four beats to the bar. If you count 1-2-3 | 1-2-3, then you are counting three beats to the bar.

Although there are four beats to the bar in 4/4 time, it does not mean that there have to be four notes to the bar. A note can be held for several beats, or more than one note can be played for a given beat. In sheet music, the length or duration of a tone is shown by different fractional written notes: whole notes, half-notes, quarter notes, eighth notes, sixteenth notes.

The most common time signatures are:

2/4 count 1-2 | 1-2 | 1-2 |
3/4 count 1-2-3 | 1-2-3 | 1-2-3 |
4/4 count 1-2-3-4 | 1-2-3-4 | 1-2-3-4 |

2/4 time, called march time, is used in much folk music and many ballads. 4/4, or common time, is the preferred beat for virtually all popular music. 3/4 time, or waltz time, is a soothing rhythm used in lullabies, romantic waltzes and folk. 3/4 time is rarely used in Rock music, but is often encountered in Country songs. It is also found in blues and jazz in compounds such as 6/8, 9/8 or 12/8 to create a feel called Swing. Traditional Jigs are in 6/8 or 12/8 time.

There are other time signatures, each with their own peculiarities and intricacies, such as 5/4, 7/4, 7/8, etc.

Beat

The beat is created by stressed and unstressed pulses. When the stress, or accent, falls on the first beat of the bar it is called the Downbeat. There can be multiple stresses in bar. A bar of 4/4 time can have one accent, 1-2-3-4, or more, 1-2-3-4. The second stress is usually not as strong as the first.

Individual beats can be subdivided. A pulse can be placed between beats, turning basic 1-2-3-4 into 1-and-2-and-3-and-4-and. Beats can be divided into triplets: 1-and-a-2-and-a-3-and-a-4-and-a. The in-between pulses are called Off-beats. More off-beats can be added for more complicated rhythms.

A song can also be syncopated, which means putting the accent on a beat other than the first beat of a bar, often the second or Backbeat, 1-2-3-4.

Syncopation is found in blues, jazz, rhythm & blues and funk. Syncopation affects the beat, but not the time – the time is still 4/4 or 12/8 whatever note the accent beat falls on.

Tempo

Tempo is how fast the piece is played, the beats per minute or the setting of the metronome. Metronomes usually have a range from 35 to 250 beats per minute; the more beats per minute, the faster the tempo. Popular songs mostly fall into a range from 100 to 135 bpm, with the majority being around 120 - 128 bpm. Slow ballads range from 80 to 100 bpm and dance tunes can go up to 140 bpm.

Rhythm and Groove

Establishing the rhythm or groove can be the most important part of a song arrangement. Getting into the groove draws the audience into the song. A groove is the combination of tempo and beat into a rhythm that gets the foot tapping and the body moving. Different rhythms are felt differently in the body. Some rhythms invite fancy footwork, some whole body shaking, some deep hip movement, other induce head banging. Because of the low frequency vibrations, bass is a very visceral instrument, you feel it as well as hear it, so groove is something you want to pay attention to in your playing.

In heavily groove-based music, the Intro is often used to establish the beat, getting the audience's bodies involved in the track before the segueing into the main song.

Approaches to Songs

Some songwriters start with a groove – they will turn on a beat box, find a groove they like and start writing over that. Other songwriters start with a melody, adding a lyric and arrangement. Others write over an interesting chord sequence; some start with a catchy hook line or musical riff and build around that; others begin with a lyric and write an accompanying melody.

The result is that different songs have a different focus and the arrangement is there to bring out this focus. For some songs it is the danceable rhythm that is most important, for others it is the message in the lyrics, for others it is the style or unique sound.

A band needs to be aware of the focus of the song and work to bring out its power. In lyric-based songs, the accompaniment tends to be a little more laid back to let the vocals take the lead. In groove based songs, the rhythm section is more prominent.

Charts and Lead Sheets

When learning new songs, bands will often use charts or lead sheets ('lead' rhymes with 'deed' as in 'to lead,' not 'dead' as in 'led'). There is no firm definition of a chart, so it can take different forms and mean different things to different people.

A basic chart often has the melody in standard notation, the lyrics and the chord changes. Charts are often found in Fake Books or Real Books. Fake Books are compilations of lead sheets of popular songs and Real Books are of jazz standards. Sometimes "lead sheet" will mean the melody shown in standard notation with the lyrics,

while the "chart" will consist of only the lyrics with the chord changes noted above.

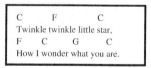

In bands with a horn section, the charts can be sheet music with parts for trumpet, sax, etc. written out. Sometimes the chords will be shown in numerical form rather than the letter names so that the piece can be played in any key:

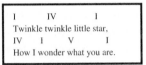

When using charts or lead sheets, the bass part must be learned by ear or improvised. There are also Fake Books and Real Books for bass, sometimes with tab notation.

Part III

Blues

Blues is a distinctive song form with its own structure and scale. The Blues is unique, often with a minor pentatonic scale played over Dominant 7th chords.

The basic form is known as the 12-Bar Blues with a I-IV-I-V-I chord progression, although there are 8-bar blues and other forms as well. Blues relies heavily on 7th chords, the V is nearly always a 7th chord and the I and IV can be 7th chords as well.

Because the basic blues progression is repetitive, blues makes extensive use of rhythmic variations, often songs are defined more by their rhythm than by their melody – a song like John Lee Hooker's *Boom Boom* is an example. Blues covers the full range of tempos, from very slow to very fast and everything in between and a large variety of beats and grooves.

The 12-bar structure means that each verse is twelve bars long with 4-beats per bar. Blues are most often in a major key, such as E, A, D or G, although there are minor Blues as well. The major chord progression would be played I for 4 bars, IV for 2 bars, I for 2 bars, V for 2 bars, then back to I for the final two bars – I-IV-I-V-I.

There can be a great deal of variety in Blues chord progressions, rhythm, tempo and melody. There are a couple of common variations on the standard 12-bar pattern. One is the Quick Change, where a IV chord is inserted into the first four bars with I for two bars, IV for one bar and back to the I for the fourth bar before changing to the IV – I-IV-I-IV-I-V-I.

Another variation, which made its way into early rock 'n roll, has a IV inserted in the final four bars after the V. The V is played for one bar, then the IV has one bar before returning to the I for two bars – I-IV-I-V-IV-I.

There are many different styles of Blues—Delta Blues, Memphis Blues, Chicago Blues, Country Blues, Jump Blues, Folk Blues, Swamp Blues, etc. Blues influence is extensive and has given inspiration to many modern musical styles such as Blues Rock, Rock and Roll, Rockabilly, Boogie-Woogie, Boogie Rock, Rhythm & Blues, Soul, Funk, Jazz and even orchestral music as in George Gershwin's *Rhapsody in Blue* and the opera *Porgy & Bess*.

Blues makes extensive use of the 'blue notes': flatted 3rd and flatted 5th and flatted 7th notes. These notes give us the Blues Scale, 1-♭3-4-♭5-5-♭7. The song *Sunshine of Your Love* by Cream uses the Blues Scale.

Blues Lyrics

Traditionally, the first line in a Blues song is repeated twice with a third line completing the verse, in a call and answer format with the first lines asking a question or posing a problem which is answered in the last line. An example is Robert Johnson's *Sweet Home Chicago*. The lyrics usually include a tag line, which is often the title.

Blues lyrics rely heavily on stories, usually about relationships, as in Etta James' *I'd Rather Go Blind*. Although there are many sad Blues songs, there is also a lot of humor in the modern Blues form.

Shuffle and Swing

Swing feel is a rhythm using swung eighth notes. This means that each beat is divided into triplets, 1-and-a-2-and-a-3-and-a-4-and-a, then the middle pulse is left out, 1- -a-2- -a-3- -a-4- -a, giving a bump – ba-bump – ba-bump – ba-bump rhythm. In Blues this feel is called the Shuffle. There is a slight difference between Swing and Shuffle. In Shuffle, the second note is held for twice as long as the first note, a 1:2 ratio, but in Swing the swung eighth notes are a little longer. You can hear the shuffle in Eric Clapton's version of Freddy King's *I'm Tore Down*, and you can hear the Swing in Benny Goodman's *In the Mood*. Most blues are in 4/4 time, but shuffle and swing can be in 12/8 time.

Syncopation

We can't talk about Blues without talking about syncopation. Syncopation means putting the beat emphasis somewhere other than the expected beat. When the accented beat is on the first note of the bar is called the downbeat, so a syncopated rhythm will put the accent on the off-beats, the backbeat or the upbeat. Syncopation is used in blues, jazz, ragtime, funk, swing, reggae and other forms, often in upbeat rhythms. Syncopation livens things up and makes songs rhythmically interesting.

You can get an idea of syncopation if you first count **1**-2-**3**-4 with the strong accent on the 1 and a weaker accent 3, as it is in most popular music in 4/4 time. Now count 1-**2**-3-**4**, with the strong accent on the 2 and the weaker accent 4 for a syncopated rhythm.

A good example of syncopation is *The Entertainer* by Scott Joplin – more ragtime than blues, but it lets you hear the syncopated rhythm.

Turnaround & Tag

Blues songs often use turnarounds between verses, little instrumental phrases that resolve from the end of one verse to the beginning of the next.

"Everything is connected."

Index

ABOUT THE AUTHOR

John C. Goodman is a bass player and a Pushcart Prize nominated writer. He has published four collections of poetry and two novels (one of which was short-listed for an Arthur Ellis Award), as well as the non-fiction work *Poetry: Tools & Techniques.*

Printed in Great Britain
by Amazon